JESUS

CW00588064

THE HEALER

Jesus the Healer

Michael Harper

■ Highland ■

British Library Cataloguing-in-Publication Data.
A catalogue record for this book is available
from the British Library

Copyright © 1986 by Michael Harper

Originally published by Hodder & Stoughton Publishers.
This edition published in 1992 by Highland Books,
an imprint of Inter Publishing Services (IPS) Ltd,
Williams Building, Woodbridge Meadows,
Guildford, Surrey GU1 1BH.

All rights reserved.
No part of this publication may be reproduced or
transmitted in any form or by any means, electronic or
mechanical, including photocopy, recording or any
information storage and retrieval system, without
either prior permission in writing from the publisher
or a licence permitting restricted copying.

In the United Kingdom such licences are issued
by the Copyright Licensing Agency,
33–35 Alfred Place, London WC1E 7DP.

Printed and bound in Great Britain by
HarperCollins Manufacturing, Glasgow.

ISBN 0 946616 85 X

Contents

Editor's Preface

The healing miracles of Jesus are among the most strongly attested aspects of his ministry, and yet they tend to alienate modern Christians. Reared in a secular culture, we argue that they could not have happened, on the assumption that God does not and cannot intervene in his world. Alternatively, if we believe that the Son of God could perhaps have performed miracles, we believe that those powers died with him in the first century.

Michael Harper, a well known writer and leader in the charismatic movement, contests both these tendencies. He believes that God did intervene in his world in the person and miracles of his Son Jesus. And he believes that the same God heals today in answer to the prayer of faith. This is neither, therefore, a dull and dreary book about healings long ago, nor a credulous and excitable account of modern healings. Instead, it is a thoughtful and careful examination of the exorcisms and healings of the historical Jesus. And he gives reason for supposing that the same God is active still to heal in our fractured society and personal lives.

The healing miracles occupy a large part of the Gospel story, yet they are largely neglected or dismissed by current New Testament scholarship. I am delighted to have in the *Jesus Library* such a careful and encouraging examination of so critical an issue by one who has seen God's healing power at work today in many parts of the world.

Michael Green

Author's Preface

I should like to thank all those who have helped me in the writing of this book. To Michael Green, the editor of the *Jesus Library* series, who invited me to make this contribution to it; I am grateful to my friend Edward England, for his many encouragements, to Rob Warner, who first commissioned the book for Hodder & Stoughton, and David Wavre his successor who brought the book to completion.

To Dr Graham Scott-Brown, for many years the Director of the Shining Hospital in Nepal, for his help with chapter four, especially his comments on the disease of leprosy and the biblical interpretation of it. To a host of other people who have wanted a book on this subject, and provided helpful suggestions. And finally to my wife Jeanne for her constant help and advice, while herself in the midst of compiling a new songbook.

All biblical references are taken from the Revised Standard Version unless otherwise stated. There is a biblical index on page 189, which will enable the reader to find each healing reference easily.

Michael Harper
Stanfords, September 1985

Chapter
1

Surprised by Power

> God does not shake miracles into Nature at random as if from a pepper-pot.
>
> C. S. Lewis

After C. S. Lewis was dragged, according to his own admission, kicking and screaming into the kingdom of God, he wrote about it in a book called *Surprised by Joy*. My gradual exposure to and acceptance of healing gifts might be called, 'surprised by power'. Actually the people often responded to the miracles of Jesus in the same way. We are told that 'they were *astonished*'. They had never seen anything like it before. In his famous book *Miracles*, C. S. Lewis shows how there is nothing haphazard or arbitrary about these healings. We are not to see God scattering miracles at random as from a pepper-pot. There was a plan in everything, even if Jesus was sometimes taken by surprise. But the orderliness was not contrived. The key was not the administrative skills of Jesus. Nor was there anything necessarily logical about it. It all happened naturally, for God's ways of doing things are different from our own.

It would be nice to think that there will one day be a definitive book on healing, which will clear up all the mysteries, dissolve the problems, and provide us with 'seven easy steps to getting and keeping our healing'. If you are looking for that kind of book, this is not it. I frankly doubt whether it will ever be written. This book focuses on Jesus' healings; on what happened 2000 years ago. It should help and encourage us, but it won't do the work of the Holy Spirit for us. We need the same guidance, inspiration and power that Jesus had.

There are no easy answers. There are many mysteries. Yet
the overwhelming evidence of the healing stories, which after
all form a sizeable part of the gospels, is that the detailed
accounts are given to encourage our faith and provide some
simple models to help us develop our own healing ministry.

My own healing adventure may help, and I will be candid. I
was brought up to believe in the truth of the Bible. I have
never seriously doubted that Jesus performed all the miracles
recorded in the gospels. But it was not until 1962 that I began
to see the stories in the gospels as encouraging us to expect the
same healings today. I met Christians who believed strongly
in the power of the Holy Spirit to heal people. They did not
seem to be put off by words like 'incurable' and 'terminal'.
But I didn't have an easy passage. For many years I struggled
with my doubts, felt ashamed of them, bottled them up, and
hid them from everyone. I believed because I was meant to,
it was expected of me. I did pray publicly and openly for
the sick, *when forced to do so, when there was no way of
escaping from it, and when it was more embarrassing to
refuse to pray than it was to pray.* I had real difficulties in
believing that anything would happen. I was ashamed of my
'cover-up'.

Slowly and patiently the Lord worked. People *were* being
healed, though often I was unaware of it. For example, in
1964 I prayed for a woman with epilepsy, who never had a fit
again; but I had to wait until 1984 before I knew it! I was
particularly frightened of wheelchair cases, and avoided
praying for such people. I had to pray on one occasion for a
woman in a wheelchair. It happened somewhere in the
United States. I promptly forgot all about it. To this day I
can't remember where or when the incident took place. It is
unlikely there was any faith in my prayers. Yet twelve years
later I heard that she had been healed, because she remembered my name and told a friend of mine about it. You see
that even though I was praying for people out of a sense of
duty the Lord answered. God can and does work even when
we are sceptical. At least I believed that *others* were successful, even if I never fancied my own chances very much.

Some years ago I was attending a large healing service in California. The star that night was Kathryn Kuhlman. My critical faculties, nurtured at school and university, were well tuned and ready for action. Frankly I was not expecting anything to happen. I was finding it a struggle not to reject the whole affair as superficial showmanship, a vulgar form of show biz transferred from the secular to the Christian stage. Suddenly Kathryn announced to a crowd of several thousand people that God was healing a young man of emphysema. His lungs had been seriously damaged when he had been involved in a fire. About forty yards from where I was sitting a young man sprang to his feet and went quickly up to the platform. He was beaming from ear to ear. 'You are healed', Kathryn said, and the young man obviously believed her. 'Run down to the end of the auditorium and back', she commanded. This he proceeded to do, to the ecstatic delight of the audience. They cheered him all the way. By this time I was ready to write the whole thing off. It had clearly been rigged. The young man was an exhibitionist. He had not really been ill at all. It had been a case of mistaken identity. The cure was psychologically induced. Kathryn Kuhlman knew this young man and his case history. These were some of the possibilities which came into my mind. But a miracle – certainly not. Every kind of rational explanation bounced backwards and forwards in my brain. The possibility that we had witnessed a miracle never occurred to me.

I turned instinctively to the man sitting next to me who was a complete stranger. I asked him what he thought about it all, with a bit of a sarcastic edge to my voice. I immediately noticed that he had been deeply moved, and I was soon to know why. 'That is my boy', he said. I was taken aback. I asked him several questions, and he told me the whole story. His son had been told by the doctors that his lungs had been so badly damaged he would never be able to run again. Prior to that evening he had been unable to walk more than fifty yards without severe breathlessness. No, he was not known to Kathryn Kuhlman, who had no prior knowledge of his condition. I learned a lesson that evening – never to limit

God and never to judge people or situations by outward
impressions alone.

Through these years my faith has grown like a seed in the
ground, and the weeds of doubts have gradually been removed, making room for further growth. I have been slow
and reluctant to accept that I can be used by God as a channel
of the healing grace of Jesus Christ today. At least I know the
problems many people wrestle with. We know God *CAN* do
it, but will he? What happens if nothing happens? How
definite should we be in prayer? Should we include the safety
clause, 'if it be your will', to let us off the hook when prayer
isn't answered? When should people give up medication after
being prayed for? Should we go on praying for people when
they don't seem to be getting any better? There are many
other questions which buzz in our minds and can so easily
paralyse us when it comes to action.

This book may help to answer some of these questions. But
it won't answer them all, and if it did there would be a whole
lot more to be answered. I have the overwhelming impression
that progress in the healing ministry in most churches is slow.
In others it is almost stationary. Large numbers of people
have little or no experience of it. If this is true, then the
corollary is also true – namely that large numbers of people
are suffering unnecessarily, and God's work is hindered as a
result. Because of this many are not able to see the glory of
God and have a chance to believe.

Since 1978 I have travelled extensively in the Third World.
If what I have just said is tragic in the western world, where
medical science and treatment are available to everyone, how
much more distressing is it amongst two-thirds of the world
with few of these privileges? In Africa for example eighty
percent of people do not have access to even elementary
medical care. The questions we are seeking to answer are very
much more relevant in that context than in ours. And the
Third World scene is much closer to the atmosphere of the
earthly life and times of Jesus Christ. If only for *their* sake, we
should give close attention to the miraculous healings of
Jesus.

Actually our western world is as much in need of the healing gifts of Christ as the poorer Third World. We have our own brands of diseases, many of which are ameliorated but not cured by drugs and medical treatment. Our hospitals and clinics are full of sick people. Chronic illness abounds. Some of it we bring upon ourselves by our unhealthy life style and the stress factors which are peculiar to our western culture. Affluence can be very debilitating.

Facts or myths?

Did Jesus Christ *actually* heal people? Did an unemployed blind beggar called Bartimaeus really receive his sight instantly when he met Jesus Christ on the Jericho road? Was Jesus' friend Lazarus *literally* raised from the dead after being buried long enough for his flesh to be putrefying? Were lepers really cleansed, did the deaf hear and the dumb speak? Was the paralysed man brought to Jesus by four of his friends a real cripple, and did Jesus heal him so that he was able to walk home? Some have a quick and easy answer. The Bible is inerrant, therefore, all these stories are true. There is no further argument or problem. But there are others for whom this answer is unacceptable. They would say that the events described cannot be squared with modern scientific data. Some would say that a few of the so-called miracles were psychologically induced. The majority, however, are either the product of the over-fertile imagination of hero-worshipping disciples or carefully devised myths which were never intended to be taken literally. In between these two extremes there are other views.

Let's begin with two incontrovertible facts. The first is that a high proportion of the four gospels is given up to describing the healings of Jesus. In Mark's gospel, which most scholars believe to have been the primary source for Matthew and Luke, 209 verses out of 666 are about the miracles of Jesus, just over thirty-one percent. If we look at the first ten chapters and omit the long passion narrative, there are 200 out of 425 verses, which is about forty-seven percent. Although the proportion in the other gospels is not so high, we are bound to conclude that the writers, however we may interpret what they have written, regarded them as crucially important. It is impossible to think of the gospels without them.

John's gospel is built around what he calls 'signs', the majority of which are healing miracles. Thus we find the healings of Jesus at the heart of the fourth gospel. Anyone reading the gospels for the first time would conclude that Jesus healed the sick and that the writers regarded this ministry as a vital part of what he came to do and to teach. As A. H. McNeile has put it, 'the record of miracles was entirely in place. The total impression could not have been produced without them. It is open to anyone to refuse to say more than this, but to say less is impossible'.[1]

The second fact, which follows from this, is that for the writers of all four gospels the healings of Jesus were important enough to be extensively reported. Most scholars hold the opinion, which is explicitly stated in the fourth gospel and implicitly in the synoptics, that the gospels were written for an evangelistic purpose, namely that people might believe in the Son of God. John actually writes in his gospel that he had included the signs that his readers 'may believe that Jesus is the Christ'. The writers wanted people to believe and throw in their lot with Jesus Christ and his followers. Since the writers had the freedom to select whatever they felt right to record in their gospels, and since we must assume that they undertook this task in a responsible manner and that theirs was not a random or arbitrary selection of materials, then we can assume that these men regarded the healings of Jesus as critical to the proclamation of the gospel. We may have reasons to question whether this is true today. But in the first century the healings of Jesus were part of that gospel message, important enough to occupy a prime position in the gospel narratives.

These are two facts from which we cannot escape. First, Jesus gave a lot of his time to healing sick people, and for the writers of the four gospels this was important enough to report extensively. And, secondly, they regarded these stories as part of the Good News. The gospels were written primarily for the conversion of unbelievers, not the comfort or encouragement of the saints. At the end of Jesus' earthly life John reports him as saying, 'Did I not tell you that if you would believe you would see the glory of God?' (Jn 11:40). There is something exultant about these words. He seems to be saying, 'I told you so'. On the other hand Jesus refused to do spectacular things for their own sake when this was demanded of him by his enemies. Yet he delighted in healing sick people.

There are theological questions which it is right to ask about the healings of Jesus. We may even question whether they really took place. What we cannot question is the fact that for the gospel writers themselves, self-deceived as they may have been or naive in the light of subsequent scientific discoveries, the healings of Jesus have a message for men and women which needs to be heeded and responded to positively. Whether we can build much on the stories of events which some say never took place is a question we have to ask. The gospel writers believed them to have taken place and built a lot on what they regarded as authentic reporting of facts. In disputing these we must not drag the gospel writers down to our own level of scepticism. Part of the polemic of the gospel was that Jesus Christ healed the sick, cast out evil spirits and raised the dead. For the authors it was part of the content of the gospel, just as the forgiveness of sins was.

The parameters of our subject

It may be helpful now to make clear the parameters of our subject. Our concern is basically with the healings of Jesus, which covered a period of only about three years. What a lot was compressed into those thousand or so days! For the earliest Christians the death of Jesus, and the removal of his physical presence from this earth, far from marking the end of the healings, was the starting point of a rapid extension of that ministry to the ends of the earth. Many of us believe that it is still going on today through the faithful and obedient service of Jesus' followers all over the world. But this is not a general book on divine healing. We are going to concentrate on the healings of Jesus during that remarkable three-year period.

The second parameter we need to set up is to define what we mean by 'healings'. In our study we shall be looking at Jesus' ministry to the sick, which includes the demonised and the dead. We will not take the word 'healing' any wider than that. I want these remarkable stories to speak for themselves. The Acts of the Apostles has sometimes been called 'the fifth gospel'. In it we read of the continuing healings of Jesus through the faith and enterprise of the early church. It would be tempting to include this book in our study too. Jesus was at it again. When Peter healed the man at the gate of the temple, he attributed it to the power of the name of Jesus. Even more striking in Acts 9:34 Peter actually says to the cripple 'Aeneas, Jesus Christ heals you'. But we shall not be including these stories except as evidence of the continuing ministry of Jesus through his body the church and in the power of the Holy Spirit given at Pentecost. Basically we will be looking only at the healings of Jesus in the days of his flesh.

This is also a book about 'healings'. Although the healings of Jesus were miracles, there were other miracles he did which were not healings. Paul makes this distinction in 1 Corinthians 12 when he lists the gifts of the Holy Spirit. There is a gift of healings (notice the plural), and also of working miracles. So we will not be examining, for example, the feeding of the five thousand or Jesus' walking on the water. The whole subject of 'miracles' is controversial. We shall be looking at it, but solely in relationship to the healings of Jesus.

Why did Jesus heal the sick?

There are several answers which have been given to this question:

1. Because he was the Messiah

Although some, like Woolston[2] and Schweitzer,[3] have tried
to deny this, it seems clear that part of the messianic expectation, according to some key passages, was that he would
heal the sick. In Isaiah 53:4–5, perhaps the most important,
and certainly the best-known, messianic passage in the Old
Testament, we read of the Messiah, 'Surely he has borne our
griefs (mg sicknesses), and carried our sorrows (mg pains)
. . . and with his stripes we are healed'. Almost as important
is Isaiah 61:1–2, according to Luke quoted by Jesus himself in
Nazareth (Lk 4:18–19), and explicitly stated by him as 'fulfilled' that day. The miracles of healing were claimed by the
gospel writers as signs that the Messiah had come.

2. Because he was the Prophet

Many times in the gospels the link is made between prophetic
word and prophetic *action*, and this is in keeping with the Old
Testament prophetic tradition. The prophets were not only
those who spoke the word, they demonstrated it too, sometimes, as for example Elijah and Elisha, with healing power.
It is significant that one of the Jewish expectations was of the
return of Elijah, the healing prophet, before the day of the
Lord.

It would seem that the popular instinct of Jesus' day was to
accept someone as a prophet of God on the evidence of
supernatural power. The woman at the well in John 4 said, 'I
perceive that you are a prophet' after Jesus had revealed
knowledge about her he could only have obtained from God.
We should also include as an example of this the important
prophecy of Isaiah 11:1–5.

3. Because of his compassion

There are those who have maintained that the basic reason
why Jesus healed the sick was sheer love for people. The
gospels explicitly state this in Matthew 9:36 and 14:14. We are
told that Jesus, 'had compassion on them, and healed their

sick'. Augustine placed the power element (*potestas*) alongside the compassionate (*benignitas*).[4] Schleiermacher regarded the miracles as important only when this element
comes to the fore.[5]

4. Because he was the Son of God

This view comes over strongly in the evangelical tradition.
The healings are seen as part of the cumulative evidence of
the gospels that Jesus was not mere man, but the incarnate
Son of God. The corollary which follows is that we are not to
expect further miracles today because Jesus is no longer with
us in the flesh. The weakness of this argument is that healings
similar to those performed by Jesus come in the Old Testament and were being performed in Jesus' day by Jews and
Gentiles on a not inconsiderable scale. The fact that Jesus
healed the sick proved nothing. It was the way he healed and
the purposes for which he healed that were significant. Nevertheless we need to add that the absence of healings would
have cast doubts on Jesus' claims to be the Messiah and the
Son of God. We can say he healed the sick because he was the
Son of God, not in order to prove he was.

The truth about Jesus and the healing he gave to people
lies in all these areas, and we don't have to choose between
them. He was the Messiah, and the Messiah was to be a
healer. He was *the* prophet, and the living word was confirmed by living action, which included healing. He was love
incarnate, and love will never pass by human need and ignore
it. He was the Son of God and so possessed an anointing
(given also to his disciples) to heal people.

Healings and Christian hope

In Jesus' healings two important streams merged. Jesus'
healings were a fulfilment of prophecy and a means of bringing people to salvation, and the early church saw this instinctively and followed these lines with enthusiasm. It is interesting that the father of the modern Christian healing movement

combined these two streams also. Johann Christoph Blumhardt was born in Stuttgart in 1805, the son of the founder of the famous Basel Mission. He was, therefore, brought up in a home with a strong interest in missions. Pastor Blumhardt developed a strong eschatological basis for his views on divine healing. He believed that the main reason for the disappearance of miracles after the early centuries was the absence of what he called 'the personal Holy Ghost'. But he believed that a new wave of miracles would reach their climax with the second coming of Christ. He died in 1880 and so never witnessed the birth of the Pentecostal movement, which more than any other fulfilled the expectations he had.

We live in similar times. The focus is increasingly shifting to 'signs and wonders' and the insight that the primary concern of the New Testament, as we have seen, is that people reading it may believe in Jesus Christ.

My desire in writing this book is that people will be encouraged to believe in the power of God to heal in today's world. But more than that I want to see people possessing the new life that Jesus primarily came to give us, life with a totally new quality about it. My prayer is that this book will help people to see and believe in Jesus Christ.

I am placing the actual accounts of the healings first in the book, because I want them to speak for themselves with the minimum of comment. I have left textual questions to the commentators. Then, later in the book, we shall explore some key issues raised by the healings of Jesus.

When Jesus gave his key-note address in Nazareth, inaugurating his public ministry, he touched on what was to become the major theme of his work, that he had come to *liberate* men and women. To that theme we shall now turn.

Chapter
2

Jesus Liberates

> The healing acts of Jesus were themselves the message
> that he had come to set men free.
>
> Francis MacNutt

The motto of Pastor Blumhardt was *Jesus ist Sieger* – 'Jesus
is Conqueror'. The black evangelist Tom Skinner ended an
address to over 12,000 American students in 1970 with the
words 'proclaim liberation to the captives . . . go into all the
world and tell men they are bound mentally, spiritually and
physically – the liberator has come'. Indeed the word 'liberation' has been in the forefront for many years. Since the war
of revolution the United States has seen 'liberty' as a central
theme of its Constitution. The Statue of Liberty in New York
harbour remains the symbol of that nation. The early
American pioneers took to heart the words in the Old Testament 'proclaim liberty throughout the land' (Lev 25:10),
words which now appear on American stamps. It became the
text of revolution. In recent years the cry for liberty has been
taken up by many disadvantaged people, particularly blacks.
The Indians in North America, the Maoris in New Zealand
and the Aborigines in Australia, to quote a few cases, have
begun to seek their own rights and freedom from domination
by the powerful white majorities in those countries. In Latin
America the word 'liberation' has been linked with 'theology'
and, therefore, come to express the cry of the poor for social
and economic justice. This has found expression particularly
in the book by Gustavo Gutierrez, *A Theology of Liberation*,
first published in Spanish in Peru in 1971.[1]

The New Testament shows us how Jesus liberated men and

women from all that oppressed them. It was especially seen in terms of freedom from sickness, satanic powers and death itself. Liberation was not limited to these areas, but the fullest expression of the liberation theme was acted out and demonstrated on this particular stage. To leave these areas out is to emasculate the gospel of the kingdom.

A liberated people

When the Bible speaks of liberty a prior bondage is always implied. The major theme of liberty in the Old Testament is concerned with the people of God in their relationship to the Egyptians. The Hebrews were delivered from literal slavery, so that they could leave Egypt and enter the promised land. This story has inspired many others faced with similar situations from the Mormons and other religious fringe groups in America looking for a homeland, to the Voortrekkers of South Africa and more recently the Israelis who have set up the modern state of Israel. It is also a major argument in the theories of liberation theology. Gutierrez sees the Israelites as 'economically oppressed'.

A new kind of liberation

Jesus' style of liberation was different from that of all others. There was nothing to touch it. His key-note address, which in many ways was definitive of all that he was to do for the next three years and through the church until the end of time, was given fittingly in the synagogue of his home town, Nazareth. It was brief but powerful. After reading from Isaiah 61, he gave a one-sentence summary, 'Today this scripture has been fulfilled in your hearing' (Lk 4:21). Jesus was claiming to be the liberator. The liberator had come, and the Spirit had anointed him for the tasks that lay ahead. Henceforth captives were going to be released and the oppressed set free. Jesus' public ministry was primarily one of liberation and he

was regarded by his contemporaries as the 'liberator'. The
enemies from whom he delivered the people were Satan, sin,
death and sickness.

Jesus ignored the Zealots who hankered after national
liberation from Rome, although he did include at least one
of them among the twelve. He had come instead to overthrow 'the prince of this world', to defeat those powers of evil
which lie behind all forms of evil, whether they are personal or institutional. The strong man was to be overcome
and his prisoners released (Jn 12:31f; Mk 3:27; Lk 10:17f).
Exorcisms (e.g. Mk 3:22f) and healings (Lk 13:16) were
important aspects of this ministry of liberation. They were a
proof that the kingdom of God had come and was amongst
them.

In the next few chapters we are going to look at the healings
of Jesus as four aspects of this liberation ministry. Christ
himself appealed to these as proof positive that the kingdom
had come and was now a reality. Although Paul's writings do
not directly concern us in this book it is important to notice
that they have the very same theme running through much of
them. To the tyrants mentioned above, from whom Jesus
came to set us free, Paul adds another, the law. Paul, like
Jesus, sees these forces as destructive and out of harmony
with the purposes of God (see Rom 6:18–23; Gal 4:21–31; 1
Cor. 15:56).

Man's alienation

It is not surprising that the Jews saw the exodus as the key
event in their long and turbulent history. It was their point of
emergence to nationhood. Abraham had only lived in tents, a
nomad wandering from place to place. Now they were to be
established in a land of their own. To God they gave thanks
for their liberation and in the Passover meal annually remembered those breathtaking moments when judgement came
upon the Egyptians and liberation came to them from the
miseries of slavery. As the Jews of the first century suffered

endless humiliations and deprivations from the hands of their Roman oppressors, it would be that period in history which they would have turned to again and again. Their prayers would have been 'Lord, do it again!' Such hopes were to be dashed to the ground. Far from being set free more chains were laid upon them culminating in the horrific siege and ultimate sacking of Jerusalem by the Romans in AD70. It is this that lies behind the last question the disciples asked the Lord immediately prior to the ascension, 'Lord, will you at this time restore the kingdom to Israel?' (Acts 1:6). Jesus' answer was to point them in the direction of a new spiritual kingdom which was to make a far greater impact on society, yet which would not save Jerusalem from its first-century holocaust.

However, we should notice that the New Testament does not major on this theme, although happy to use its language. Jesus was not primarily another liberator like Moses. He was the second Adam, and it is this theme – along with the Abrahamic – which is much more prominent in the arguments of Paul, particularly in the epistle to the Romans. The New Testament takes us back to the very roots of sin and man's first acts of disobedience. It is the restoration of man not the restoration of the nation that the New Testament is primarily concerned about. The Passover is a Jewish saga, telling the story of the beginnings of Jewish exclusiveness. But the creation narrative in Genesis is more fundamental, taking us to the heart of the problem, man's first stages of rebellion and the results that followed. The creation of the nation was only a step in the general purposes of God which have always been the salvation of the entire world. Thus salvation from sin is primary, and deliverance from political enemies only secondary, in the full purposes of God. God's salvation is personal from beginning to end.

It is crucial to see this as the background to the ministry of Jesus. He came to restore men and women to a wholeness which was marred in the garden of Eden, not to new national pride and exclusiveness. It is surely no coincidence that the garden of Gethsemane figures so prominently in the story of

Jesus' passion and that the tomb in which Jesus' body was laid
and from which the same body rose on the third day, was also
in a garden, so that Mary Magdalene thought at first that Jesus
was the gardener. Here was the garden of restoration from all
the ill effects and influence of that other garden so many years
before.

In Genesis chapters 1 and 2 we see man created for
fellowship with God, just as the woman is created for fellowship with the man. God comes walking in the garden
looking for that companionship. But Adam and Eve hide
themselves from God, just as they had hidden their bodies
from themselves with fig leaves. Sin always has that effect
upon people. They are ashamed of themselves and they run
away and hide from God. The fall of man was social as well as
personal, physical as well as spiritual. Disintegration began to
take place in the midst of a creation which was in its original
state good and orderly. The harmony between God, nature
and man was profoundly disturbed. Man's banishment from
the garden was the punishment meted out to those who could
no longer be trusted. Acts of sinful disobedience were to
follow and every endeavour of man was to end in frustration
and failure.

We see all the enemies which Jesus came to do battle with
there in the garden of Eden. Man was conquered and dis-
graced. Satan had his way. Sickness began to afflict men's
bodies. Death came through Adam's one act of disobedience
and sin became an inevitable part of man's human nature.
Jesus faced these enemies from his birth in Bethlehem until
his death in Jerusalem and finally and completely overcame
them. All the powers of darkness were routed. Paul puts it
magnificently in Colossians 2:15, 'He (Jesus) disarmed the
principalities and powers and made a public example of them,
triumphing over them in him' (or probably 'it', referring to
the cross). The liberator came and conquered. He has now
called his people to be liberators as well and to proclaim this
message throughout the earth. But the message can easily be
emasculated. Many parts of the church do not proclaim it at
all. Other parts have such little faith that it comes over

weakly. Most leave out those very parts of the message which are given so much prominence in the gospels, namely the healings and deliverances. They were all part of Jesus' plan for the world's restoration; why leave any part out?

Supernatural knowledge

Before we end this chapter we need to look briefly at an important feature in Jesus' remarkable healing work. Again and again he was able to see things which were hidden from most people. He called complete strangers by name. He said to the man lowered through the roof that his sins were forgiven, when he had been brought to Jesus for healing. Jesus was able to see the whole situation, and make decisions on the basis of knowledge and information he could only have received from the Holy Spirit. At the pool of Bethesda he knew all about the one man he healed. He could read people like a book.

A growing number of people believe, as I do, that these are all examples of a gift called 'the word of knowledge', which is probably what Paul is referring to in 1 Corinthians 12:8. At all events this same ability to see and know things normally hidden from us is being experienced on an increasingly large scale today. It is of the utmost importance that we have a revelation from God concerning every possible aspect of human sickness. Is it due to human sin, and are there particular sins which need to be confessed? Are there demonic forces involved, and what are they? What mental attitudes are there which may be blocking healing? Is it God's will to heal instantly or later? Are other people involved? Jesus always knew the situation as it was, not as it seemed to be. It is said that 'he knew what was in man'. Nothing seemed to be hidden from him, and so he was able to speak with authority. It is one of the most important keys to understanding the healings of Jesus, and without it we are powerless to carry on the work that Jesus began.

In the next five chapters we shall be looking at Jesus' healings one by one. I have categorised them so that they can be seen more clearly as the fruit of Jesus' liberating ministry. We see him setting men, women and children free from satanic power, human sin, death itself and various forms of sickness. The liberator came and is still with us in the power and presence of the Holy Spirit.

Chapter
3

Satan Is Defeated

We must wage irreconcilable war with him who con-
spires man's ruin.

John Calvin

Jesus Christ's coming was a head-on confrontation with
satanic powers. His ministry included exorcisms or deliverances. Part of the pattern of liberation, prophesied in Isaiah
61 and fulfilled by Christ, was to overthrow or neutralise the
power of the devil. The word often translated 'destroy' (e.g.
in 1 Jn 3:8) really means to neutralise or render powerless.
According to the gospel writers sickness and human disability
were sometimes directly attributable to satanic power. Thus if
healing was to take place Satan's power and authority would
first need to be broken. This Jesus did on a number of
occasions, and later commissioned his disciples to do the same
in his name. Although there is no mention of deliverance
ministry in the fourth gospel, the reader is left in no doubt as
to the extent and importance of the spiritual warfare which
was being waged ceaselessly between Christ and Satan. Jesus
was twice accused of having a devil (Jn 7:20 and 8:48), and on
another occasion it was said of him, 'he has a demon' (Jn
10:20). Jesus' answer was to turn the accusation in the other
direction, 'you are of your father, the devil', he said to them
(Jn 8:44). During the last supper John tells us that it was the
devil who had put it into the heart of Judas to betray his
master (Jn 13:2), and at that critical moment Satan entered
into Judas (13:27).

More healings of Jesus are related to satanic influence than
any other single factor, and some of these stories are amongst

the most vivid and important in the New Testament. I have listed eight healings which are in this category. It is important also to notice that Jesus, having demonstrated to his disciples the effectiveness of his deliverance ministry, sent them off to do the same. In Luke 9:1ff the twelve were given power and authority 'over all demons'. In Luke 10:1ff the seventy (or seventy-two) are given authority to 'heal the sick'. On that occasion Jesus made no reference to deliverance, and did not officially commission them for it. But apparently they didn't need to be told. The thing that excited them most was that 'the demons are subject to us in your name' (v.17). Jesus did not rebuke them for exceeding their powers, but affirmed their authority 'to tread upon serpents and scorpions, and over all the power of the enemy' (v. 19). It is true that he had to dampen somewhat their enthusiasm for demon-chasing by telling them that they ought to be rejoicing much more at their place on the heavenly register. But Jesus then turned to the Father and praised him that he had 'hidden these things from the wise and understanding and revealed them to babes' (v. 21). It is likely that Jesus would have been thinking especially of their deliverance ministry when he referred to the 'these things'.

Something lost

For many years now Christian liberalism has undermined the church's acceptance of the reality of Satan and, therefore, its confidence in the victory of Jesus Christ over all these powers. Gerald Heard has written 'Newton banished God from nature, Darwin from life and Freud has banished him from his last stronghold, the soul.' Newton allowed no room for irrational principles in nature, and the devil's conspiracy against God and his people lay in just such a realm. For Darwin the biological struggle superseded that with demonic forces. For him the struggle for existence, the survival of the fittest, was to be biologically not spiritually understood. Freud took the retreat from the recognition of spiritual warfare a stage further. The powers of darkness were dissolved by him into various complexes and neuroses. The fight of faith was no longer with spiritual forces of satanic origin, it was now a matter of inner individual adjustment. Satan was simply an invention of human intellect to explain the problems of good and evil.

Many people take the view that belief in demon possession is untenable today because of the discoveries of modern psychiatry. It is now regarded as a mental disorder which fits into one of the various categories psychiatrists have delineated. The argument is that since modern psychiatry can explain the phenomenon we no longer need to believe in evil spirits. McCasland maintains this position in his book *By the Finger of God*.[1] We need to reject such logic. Psychiatry is rarely able to explain mental disorder but only to describe it. John Wilkinson writes about this: 'psychiatry deals with descriptions more than causes . . . the term demon possession defines a cause of mental disease and is in a different category from the descriptive terminology with which modern psychiatry works'.[2] Thus the Gadarene demoniac could be described as suffering from a manic-depressive psychosis. That is simply describing his disorder, it says nothing about the causes of it. The causes matter most, and if healing is to come, then a proper diagnosis here is essential.

In a perceptive article in the *Scottish Journal of Theology*, James Stewart summed up his concern with these words, 'We have lost Paul fighting with wild beasts at Ephesus, and Luther flinging his ink-pot at the devil.'[3] The main point of his article is that the cross is emptied of much of its power and significance if the reality of satanic powers goes unrecognised, 'the drama [of the cross] can be understood only when the New Testament teaching on the invisible cosmic powers – *exousia, archontes, stoicheia* and the like is taken seriously'.[4]

We are faced with two possibilities: either there are no such things as demons or evil spirits, and the whole of the battle between good and evil is between God and man. Or there are other intelligent beings which are neither human nor divine (except in a fallen sense), and which carry on a malevolent campaign against God and his people. We need to recognise that both views are difficult to accept. All our western thinking based on human rationality reacts strongly to any suggestion of evil spiritual forces which plot man's overthrow and work invisibly against all God's work in the world. But it is equally difficult to believe that man has a monopoly of all the undoubted evil in this world, and that he alone is accountable. 'How could they have done it?' is a frequent exclamation when some new horror story comes to light revealing another example of the depravity of human behaviour. When this kind of thing happens it seems inconceivable that the only factors involved are human. Whichever view is right, one can hardly stress enough the importance of coming to a right opinion, because if a large part of the church is deceived as to the origins and extent of evil and how to combat it, it will not be in touch with reality and will be easily deceived.

The coming of Jesus to this earth, according to eyewitness accounts recorded by the writers of the New Testament, was an advance into enemy held territory. Only in this way could these massive spiritual forces be neutralised.

The temptations of Jesus set the stage for so much of what was to follow. In a sense they were the story of his life. When the disciples went out alone and began to master Satan and his demonic forces, Jesus told the disciples, 'I saw Satan fall like lightning from heaven' (Lk 10:18). As Jesus approached his hour of trial and death he told his disciples, 'Now is the judgment of this world, now shall the ruler of this world be cast out' (John 12:31). According to Paul, Jesus at the cross 'disarmed the principalities and powers' (Col 2:15). P. T. Forsyth saw the holiness of Christ in his death as the one thing 'damnatory to the Satanic power'. He writes, 'It was His death which consummated that holiness. It was His death, therefore, that was Satan's fatal doom.'[5] In his book, *The Glorious Gospel*, Forsyth describes Satan after Calvary as 'a bull in a net', a chained beast kicking himself to death. And James Stewart concludes his article (mentioned earlier) by saying that it is no good setting a tepid Christianity against a scorching paganism, 'the only way to meet that demonic mystic passion is with the *dunamis* and passion of the Lord.'[6] Only the Holy Spirit can conquer unholy spirits.

The church needs to recover its understanding and experience of this spiritual dimension. It is my conviction that many people are prisoners of these evil powers and that they affect our lives physically, emotionally and spiritually far more than most people are prepared to admit. They also extend into many areas of national and international life. (The rise and development of terrorism in the world is only one of many examples one could give.) They are surely an important explanation of entrenched evil which corrupts society and blinds millions of people to the ultimate reality in Jesus Christ. Some will still disagree, and even smile at all this. But the truth of what I am saying can be seen in the lives of thousands who have been set free from these powers, just as others were so successfully freed by Jesus during the years of his ministry on earth.

Exorcism or deliverance?

In this chapter I am deliberately describing Jesus' ministry as one of 'deliverance'. In the New Testament we see Jesus as the liberator rather than Jesus as an exorcist. In recent years, particularly through the influence of the film *The Exorcist*, this word has become popular and, as it always tends to be, has been confused with much on the fringes of occultism or with mumbo-jumbo which is a far cry from the ministry of Jesus himself. This is one of the reasons why I have avoided the use of the word for many years. There was similar confusion in Jesus' day. The Jews then had many famous exorcists, and their work extended throughout the Roman empire.

But Jesus' method was quite different from that of the Jewish exorcists. Jesus cast out demons 'with a word' (Mt 8:16), not by magic incantations, which was the Jewish method. James Dunn sees in this ministry of Jesus 'something wholly distinctive, indeed *unique*, about his consciousness of power'.[7] Exorcism itself is barely mentioned by Paul and is not listed amongst either the gifts or the ministries of the Holy Spirit. In Acts the only exorcists mentioned are Jewish and they came to a sticky end when they plagiarised the name of Jesus (Acts 19:13–17). The use of the name of Jesus by Jewish exorcists was being practised even earlier according to Mark 9:38. Jesus' tolerant response was to allow them to carry on.

But the importance of this ministry, whatever word we may use for it, is clear in church history. Harnack speaks of Christians using this ministry and of it forming 'one very powerful method of their mission and propaganda . . . Christians had command of weapons which were invincible'.[8] Alan Richardson sees the setting of people free from the fear of demons as an important element in the successful conquest of the other religions of the ancient world.[9] So Christians rapidly ousted the Jewish exorcists from their position of supremacy.

Satan's rise and fall

There is no elaborate doctrine of demonism in the Old Testament, although satanic influence is mentioned on a number of occasions. Both in Babylonia and Egypt there was strong belief in such evil powers and experience of them. In fact wherever the Israelites went there was much spiritual warfare against evil spirits. In Egypt Moses took on the magicians who competed with him with their secret arts (Ex 8:7, etc). In Canaan there was open conflict on a number of occasions, notably when Saul sought the help of the so-called witch of Endor and when Elijah confronted the prophets of Baal on Mount Carmel. This influence was extended as the Israelites experienced the bitterness of exile in Babylon and later when they were exposed to the Greek invasions and then the Roman occupation. After the exile belief in and experience of evil spirits increased, as did the ministry of exorcism.

We know that Jewish Rabbis believed that diseases were caused by demons, which they named after the particular kind of disease which was afflicting the person. The existence of demons is one thing, the extent to which they influence and affect people is another. Undoubtedly in both biblical times and in church history ever since, there have been times when people have taken an exaggerated interest in the demonic. This was particularly true in the Middle Ages when many sicknesses such as coughing and catarrh were attributed to demons. There were also quasi-magical formulae invented for cures, including blood, holy water, and the wearing of amulets. Superstition abounded in those days, and the fear of demons, from which Jesus had delivered mankind, reasserted itself with sometimes disastrous results.

Since Satan's defeat at Calvary his rise to prominence and his power to influence has largely been possible because of Christian unfaithfulness and ignorance. C. S. Lewis put it well when he wrote in his famous book *The Screwtape Letters*, 'There are two equal and opposite errors into which our race can fall about the devils. One is to disbelieve in their existence. The other is to believe, and to feel an excessive and unhealthy interest in them. They themselves are equally pleased by both errors and hail a materialist or a magician with the same delight.'[10] There is no doubt where western materialism has driven us. The wholesale rejection of belief in evil spirits, gifted with sense and intelligence, is as unhealthy as the Middle Ages' preoccupation with them. The Reformation reaction poured the baby out with the bathwater. Our own modern reactions can be equally unfortunate.

In the end we should accept the authority of Jesus Christ himself. We are referring to what James Dunn calls 'the base-rock historicity of the gospels'.[11] Deliverances were the one group of miracles to which D. F. Strauss attached the highest probability of historical accuracy in his famous book on the mythical nature of the miracle stories in the gospels.[12] Bultmann and Dibelius have taken a similar position.[13] For us to accept the reality of this spiritual warfare today demands faith and confidence in Jesus Christ which is in short supply in our western churches. Archbishop Trench wrote many years ago of the veracity of Christ and his teaching, that if we assume 'there was no Satan at all . . . what should we have here for a King of truth?'[14] We need to avoid both the Manichaean error that evil is eternal and therefore a god, and the pantheism that denies any reality to evil at all. The world is not a chessboard on which God plays both sides at once. Jesus would never have used language which would have upheld and confirmed so serious a potential error in the minds of men as the belief in satanic influences, if they did not in truth exist.

Healings and diagnosis

In the last hundred years there has been a massive advance in medical knowledge. This has been accomplished on many fronts. It has coincided with the in-roads of liberalism in biblical studies which has cast doubts on the truth of the healings of Jesus. It is not surprising that the convergence of these two should have influenced the interpretation of the accounts of the healing ministry of Jesus Christ. Attempts have been made to explain away the miraculous element which pre-scientific writers have presumed in their narratives. Thus physical and medical explanations have been made which have cast serious doubts on the reliability of these stories.

The rapid advance of psychology and psychiatric medicine have also had their repercussions on the debate. Thus the word 'psychosomatic' has been introduced to describe these influences on the human body, and not a few of the miracle stories have been attributed to psychological causes. It was E. R. Micklem in his book *Miracles and the New Psychology* who pioneered this new approach, and Leslie Weatherhead continued along the same lines.[15] Micklem set out to prove that healing, as recorded in the Bible and experienced today, was not contrary to the medical and psychological knowledge of his day; he believed that there were many indications of exact parallels.

Although this is a fascinating road to travel, it is one which this writer feels ill-equipped to pass down. In any case the Christian world is no longer under siege by scientific knowledge to the extent it was. Neither the sciences of medicine or psychology have provided all the answers, and indeed doubts are being universally expressed about many scientific dogmas. They provide part of the picture, but not the whole. No longer is there the urgency to answer scientific questions about the healings attributed to Jesus Christ, and I am certainly not competent to attempt to do so. As I am not a doctor I will not try to give medical explanations or diagnoses of these healings. If you are wanting good suggestions from a Christian doctor I would recommend John Wilkinson's book *Health and Healing*.[16]

We now proceed to our treatment of Jesus' healings and shall examine them one by one. In each chapter, the healings will be listed with the biblical references. Then there will be comments on the salient features of each story. There will be no attempt to provide a full exegesis for each healing, nor to tackle the textual problems unless they bear significantly on the stories themselves. For these the reader should turn to the relevant commentaries of which there are many for each of the gospels.

Here is the list of the healings we shall be looking at in this chapter:

1. The devil in the synagogue (Mk 1:21–28; Lk 4:31–37).
2. Deliverance in a cemetery (Mt 8:28–34; Mk 5:1–20; Lk 8:26–39).
3. The one they couldn't heal (Mt 17:14–21; Mk 9:14–29; Lk 9:37–43).
4. A dumb man speaks (Mt 9:32–34).
5. A blind and dumb man healed (Mt 12:22–24).
6. A woman has seven demons expelled (Lk 8:1–3).
7. Deliverance at a distance (Mt 15:21–28; Mk 7:24–30).
8. The woman with the bent back (Lk 13:10–17).

1. The devil in the synagogue
   Mk 1:21–28; Lk 4:31–37

Both Mark and Luke regard this story as very important. For
them it was the first visible sign that the kingdom of God had
come in the person of Jesus Christ. The fact that it took place
in a synagogue was also significant. Here was Jesus rooting
out evil in the religious establishment. He did in the synagogue what he was later to do in the temple, casting out what
did not belong there.

At first sight it seems surprising that there should have been
a man in a synagogue with an unclean spirit (Lk, 'the spirit of
an unclean demon'). He had probably been coming there for
many years. When we consider that demonic beings are
spiritual why should we be surprised if they thrive in religious
settings? It seems clear that this unclean spirit had been lying
dormant for a long time, and it was the power and authority,
first of Jesus' presence, and then his word, which flushed it
out. It seems from this story, as well as others, that demonic
powers could not keep still or silent in the presence of one like
Jesus, upon whom the anointing power of the Holy Spirit
rested. What happened on this occasion is comparatively
common in times of great movements of the Holy Spirit. The
presence of the Holy Spirit in the life of a Christian can
provoke and expose the enemy in a clear and demonstrable
fashion.

We need also to note the dual reference to authority in
Mark 1:22, 27. Jesus had no need to assert his credentials. It is
true these were later to be challenged by the Jewish authorities. ('By what authority are you doing these things, or who
gave you this authority to do them?', they said (Mk 11:28).)
But in this story the crowd itself, the synagogue congregation,
recognised that Jesus had authority in what he said in his
teaching (v. 22) and what he did in his ministry of deliverance
(v. 27); 'With authority he commands even the unclean
spirits, and they obey him.' It is important to see the two
aspects of Jesus' authority. It was evident when he taught, for
many said that he spoke with authority. So also when Jesus

healed sick people, the crowds had a visual aid or demonstration of the teaching he had given them about the kingdom of God. This pattern was to continue throughout the earthly life of Jesus, and later in the early church as evidenced by examples in the Acts of the Apostles. It is of vital importance that we notice these two aspects of authority. The church today needs *both – the authority of the word*, God speaking, and *the authority of actions*, God doing. Alas it often lacks both.

We should notice that the demonic voice speaks in the plural – 'what have you to do with *us*, Jesus of Nazareth?' (Mk 1:24). The same pattern is followed in the story of the madman in the cemetery of the Gerasenes – 'for *we* are many' (Mk 5:9). This may have been a sinister equivalent of the royal 'we' or an indication that demons usually work in teams.

Notice also the absence of magic or superstitious trimmings. Jesus stands no nonsense. He rebukes the evil spirit, commands it to be silent (he does not allow false witnesses to confess him) and commands it immediately to leave this man. The results are dramatic and spontaneous.

We see here too the action of one who claimed absolute authority in the spiritual world, and got results to substantiate such claims. Angels and apostles rebuke too, but in the name of another (Jude 9, Acts 16:18). Jesus Christ does so in his own name and by his own right.

The most striking feature in this story is the confession the unclean spirit makes of Christ as 'the Holy One of God' (Mk 1:24). In Luke's version it is even more significant because it comes immediately after the denial of Christ in Nazareth and the assassination attempt on Jesus' life. There he literally 'came to his own home, and his own people received him not' (Jn 1:11). Yet shortly afterwards an evil spirit is confessing Christ in the synagogue of Capernaum, regarded as a particularly evil city (see Lk 10:15). The contrast between the two events is meant to be noticed. The gospels are full of such surprises; men deny Jesus Christ while devils accept him!

Finally, there is an interesting reference in the text to the actual moment of deliverance. Mark tells us that the unclean

spirit convulsed the man and cried with a loud voice (1:26);
Luke says the demon threw him 'down in the midst' and adds
'having done him no harm' (4:35). Those today who have had
experience of a ministry of deliverance report similar happenings. Satan often fiercely buffets those who are in the act of
being delivered from his power for ever.

2. Deliverance in a cemetery
Mt 8:28–34; Mk 5:1–20; Lk 8:26–39

This is one of two healings from demonic influence which are
recorded in all the synoptic gospels. In many ways it is the
most important yet most perplexing of them all.

It is not the purpose of this book to examine textual
problems, though there is fertile ground for much speculation. Because the text raises such problems many scholars
have rejected the story. Dibelius and Bultmann believe it to
have profane Jewish origins.[17] Schmiedel deserves full marks
for originality when he speculates that Paul was the demoniac
mentioned in the story![18]

The question of the pigs raises ethical questions. Jesus did
not actually cast the spirits into the pigs. Aquinas comments
'But that the swine were driven into the sea was no mark of
the divine miracle, but was the work of the devils by divine
permission.'[19] If they were Jewish owners, were they being
punished for breaking the law? These are questions which can
be endlessly debated. Though pigs were unclean to Jews they
were revered in pagan rites. Were the owners of these pigs
Jews or Gentiles? We are not told. But let's get away from
superficial speculation about the details and see what we can
learn from the story itself.

Of greater importance than the details of the story is the
setting in which it is told. All three gospels are agreed that
the occasion of the storm on the lake, when Jesus' life
was threatened and the storm was stilled by his authority,
took place immediately before this particular healing. The
disciples were in a state of shock as they came ashore

having narrowly escaped death. Mark paints the picture clearly. It was Jesus who said to the disciples 'Let us go across to the other side' (4:35), no doubt sensing that there was something important to do when they got there. But in between lay the lake, and an incident which put them at great risk. We know too from Mark's account that once the demoniac had been healed the disciples got into their boats and sailed back across the lake. In other words the sole reason for their crossing the lake at the risk of their lives was to heal a man who had been utterly rejected by a society powerless to do anything for him. This teaches us much about the compassion of Christ, his obedience to divine guidance, and the worth of every individual created in the image of God, however depraved they may be.

The positioning of these two stories next to one another has its own message. The Jesus who stilled the storm on the lake, and took authority over the elements, also took authority over the storm in this man's life. The picture of him sitting beside Jesus and the disciples 'clothed and in his right mind, the man who had had the legion' (Mk 5:15) is one of the most touching and dramatic in all the gospels. No wonder the onlookers were scared to death. It must have been an awesome moment.

The question of the fate of the pigs should be held in proportion. The fear which this incident brought to the community only shows that they were more concerned about their financial loss than the health of their fellow citizen. We have to be careful not to make the same false judgement if we overemphasise the superficial textual problems and miss the greatness of what happened and the joy this healing must have brought, not only to the man himself, but to all his family and friends. A society which rates pigs of greater value than human life is in trouble.

We need also to notice something the possessed man says. When Jesus asked him the question 'What is your name?' he replied, 'My name is Legion; for we are many' (Mk 5:9). Were there two voices or one? Did the man say 'My name is Legion' and another sinister being add 'for we are many'?

Those who have had experience of similar cases know of
people speaking with two different voices, the normal one
and another voice altogether. This is a likely explanation of
this strange sentence.

As we leave this story we notice that the usual restraint that
Jesus placed on those healed, to tell no one about it, is in this
instance lifted. On the other side of the lake people are told to
keep the news of their healing to themselves and to share it
with no one. Not so in this case. 'Go home to your friends,'
Jesus says, 'and tell them how much the Lord has done for
you, and how he has had mercy on you' (Mk 5:19). The
location may well be the explanation for this change of
principle.

In a real sense this man had so profoundly experienced the
coming of the kingdom, he could be trusted to be a faithful
witness, and Jesus, who was about to leave this area never to
return, would be safe from all the problems of mob adulation.

3. The one they couldn't heal
   Mt 17:14–21; Mk 9:14–29; Lk 9:37–43

This is the second healing through deliverance which is
recorded in all the synoptic gospels. It also comes in the same
order in each, between the story of the transfiguration and the
second prediction of Jesus' death. There are slight variations
in the texts. In Matthew the man's son is called an 'epileptic',
in Mark he is said to have a dumb spirit, and in Luke simply 'a
spirit' which seizes him.

The link with the transfiguration is an obvious one; perhaps
we are meant to see reminiscences of Moses on the mountain.
The leaders are temporarily absent. Jesus had been on the
mountain with Peter, James and John. Things would have
turned out differently had they been with the others. We can
also imagine the contrast between the peace and glory up on
the mountain and the battle on the plains between the power
and grace of God and demonic forces bent on destroying the
life of a young boy. Mark tells us that the scribes were arguing

with them (presumably the nine disciples, Mk 9:14). They were obviously pressing their advantage due to the absence of Jesus. The Marcan version abounds with graphic and telling details.

It would seem certain that in these circumstances the rebuke Christ delivers, 'O faithless generation . . .', was delivered to the crowd in general and the scribes in particular. It is inconceivable that Jesus would have publicly shamed the disciples in the presence of the scribes by rebuking them. The probability was that the disciples had made the mistake of arguing with the scribes while at the same time seeking to minister to the young boy, which is normally a fatal combination. Chrysostom says that Jesus excluded the disciples from this stern condemnation and that it was only intended for the large crowd which had gathered to see what was going on.[20] It is probable that both were to some extent included. The phrase 'O faithless generation' could only really apply to the crowd, whereas the words 'how long am I to be with you?' must have included the disciples. But his primary target was surely the scribes and the unbelieving element in the crowd.

We are also told what Jesus said to the disciples in private. There is a textual variation in Matthew 17:20. Some manuscripts read 'unbelief' (*apistian*), others 'little faith' (*oligopistian*). It is much more likely that Jesus told the disciples their failure was due to 'little faith' than to 'unbelief'. In the gospels the disciples were often charged with having 'little faith' (e.g. Mt 6:30; 8:26; 14:31; 16:8) but never (apart from Thomas in Jn 20:27) with having none. It is easy to judge Jesus' relationship to the disciples as at times harsh, even cynical. But that was not so; in this story he is shielding them from humiliation at the hands of the scribes and from public embarrassment. In private he is correcting them and teaching them the reasons for their failure.

The description of this person's disease and deliverance is particularly graphic in all three gospels. In Matthew the father comments that his son 'suffers terribly; for often he falls into the fire, and often into the water' (17:15). Mark records the father saying 'wherever it seizes him, it dashes him down; and he foams and grinds his teeth and becomes rigid' (9:18). Luke tells us he was an only child and that 'he suddenly cries out; it convulses him till he foams, and shatters him, and will hardly leave him' (9:39). The deliverance itself is described in some detail. In Matthew there is a simple statement, 'the demon came out of him' (17:18). Mark, however, tells us that there was an immediate reaction when the boy was brought to Jesus: 'when the spirit saw him, immediately it convulsed the boy, and he fell on the ground and rolled about, foaming at the mouth' (9:20). Then, when Jesus spoke the words of deliverance, including the words, 'never enter him again' we are told that the boy cried out and was convulsed terribly and 'was like a corpse' so that most of those watching thought he was dead (vv. 25, 26). Luke also tells us that 'the demon tore him and convulsed him' (9:42). Then we are told that Jesus rebuked the unclean spirit, presumably to prevent it causing further harm, and 'healed the boy' giving him back to his father.

The details given are a further indication of the reliability of the records. They ring true, and indeed are often matched today in the experience of those involved in this kind of ministry. There has always been a primitive aversion to epilepsy and the Jews regarded it as a particularly malignant disease. In examining the details we notice again the compassion of Jesus Christ, the authority with which he faces the situation, and the concern he shows for the father, who must have been upset that his son had become the subject of theological controversy rather than the object of loving care.

Mark's description is so graphic it suggests the writer was an eyewitness. He records for us the famous conversation with the father, who clearly believed that Jesus could do something even though the disciples had failed. Jesus picks up the tiny flame of faith and fans it rather than quenches it. 'If you can!', he says, 'All things are possible to him who believes' (9:23). The man rises to this – 'I believe; help my unbelief!' We see Jesus like a spiritual midwife concerned to deliver 'faith' in this man. But what we mainly notice in this man is that when faith is born it serves to reveal the hidden areas of unbelief.

Just as the most godly people are most aware of ungodliness in themselves, so the most faithful know their own weakness and faithlessness more clearly than those who don't believe.

There is a well-known gloss in Mark 9:29, 'This kind cannot be driven out by anything but prayer and fasting.' The last two words are missing in some of the best manuscripts and seem almost certainly to have been a later ascetically inclined addition. Clearly in this instance there would have been no time for fasting either for the disciples or Jesus himself. Nevertheless we do learn from this verse that there seem to be different kinds of evil spirits, some more powerful than others. In other words there is a hierarchy of hell as well as a hierarchy of heaven. The prayer on the mountain of transfiguration would have been ideal preparation for this powerful deliverance. Luke gives us a beautiful description of the reaction of the crowd, 'all were astonished at the majesty of God' (9:43).

We must not deduce from this story that all epilepsy is caused by demonic powers. But we should be open to this possibility without putting moral blame for the condition on the sufferer.

4. A dumb man speaks
   Mt 9:32–34

We now come to two cases which are only recorded for us in Matthew's gospel. In the first, a man was brought to Jesus who was dumb because of demonic activity. We need to notice the frequent references to satanic attacks in the area of the senses. Deafness would prevent a person hearing the word of God and dumbness from speaking it. We should not, therefore, be surprised to read of deaf and dumb people needing to be set free from satanic power.

Loos says of this incident that it reveals 'the absolutely unique manner in which Jesus healed the sick and the possessed'.[21] The crowd's response was, 'Never was anything like this seen in Israel' (v. 33). Jesus was by no means unique in what he was doing. The Graeco-Roman world abounded in faith healers and the Jews had their exorcists everywhere. Yet the way he did it, and the results he achieved were unique in Israel. His enemies could not deny what he was doing, only the source from which he gained his power.

5. A blind and dumb man healed
   Mt 12:22–24

This story is similar to the preceding one and evoked a response which is much the same. What is interesting about this case is that although Matthew is specific in describing the man as a 'blind and dumb demoniac' there is no mention of deliverance ministry as such. We are simply told that Jesus 'healed him'. In other words there is no mention of the expulsion of demons. This would justify our treating such cases as part of the healing ministry of Jesus. Actually, his opponents clearly considered this a 'deliverance' because they accuse Jesus of casting out demons by 'the prince of demons'. Jesus in his answer to their comments talks about casting out demons which would also indicate that he regarded the issue as being closely involved with the meaning and understanding of deliverance.

6. A woman has seven demons expelled
   Lk 8:1–3

This record is unique to Luke and reveals his concern to show Jesus' high regard for women in the increasingly close-knit band of his disciples. The twelve are mentioned 'and also some women who had been healed of evil spirits and infirmities'. Mary Magdalene is particularly singled out as the one 'from whom seven demons had gone out' although probably other women in the group had been similarly delivered. Notice that Luke uses the phrase 'healed of evil spirits', yet another example of a deliverance being described as a healing. In Mark 16:9 there is another reference to Mary Magdalene, 'from whom he had cast out seven demons', it would seem that this healing was well known throughout the apostolic band. The number 'seven' need not be taken literally. It is the number of totality and, therefore, might be saying that this woman was completely in Satan's grip. It is not known for certain if she was a former prostitute. Loos quite rightly points out that 'we nowhere read that "possession was related to special sinfulness"'.[21] This woman must have been eternally grateful to the Lord for all that he had done for her. No wonder she, with the other woman, 'provided for them out of their means'.

7. Deliverance at a distance
   Mt 15:21–28; Mk 7:24–30

The story of the healing of the Canaanite woman is the only case recorded in the gospels of someone being liberated from demons at a distance. In every other instance the ministry takes place on the spot. Jesus on this occasion does not go to the young girl, yet we are told she was healed instantly (Mt 15:28). As such it is an interesting exception.

The Matthean version is the fuller and more graphic. The conversation between Jesus and the woman raises several issues. Some see Jesus as dealing harshly and insensitively with her, although later he gives her the accolade 'great is your faith'.

It is at first sight surprising that Jesus should speak of his ministry as exclusively 'to the lost sheep of the house of Israel' (Mt 15:24), for there were other exceptions to this rule, notably his healing of the centurion's servant, although the servant may himself have been Jewish.

The woman's response to Jesus is one of the classics of the New Testament, 'even the dogs eat the crumbs that fall from their master's table' (15:27). We need to remember that dogs were not domesticated in those days except in Greece. Jeremias writes that we need to 'think of the contempt in

which dogs are held in the East, where they are a plague'.[22]
The Talmud speaks of dogs as 'most despised, the most
impertinent and the most wretched of creatures'.[23]

This woman found her way into the heart of Jesus. Trench
comments, 'she takes the sword out of his own hand, with
which to overcome Him'.[24] Luther puts it, 'she snares Christ
in his own words'.[25] On any showing it was brilliant repartee.
It reminds us of Jacob wrestling with God. Jesus again
recognised the genuineness of the faith that was present in
this woman, so instead of crushing it he drew it out of her. Did
he know what she was going to say and so gave her her head
and deliberately played into her hands?

In this story we see faith advancing step by step and
overcoming the human barriers one by one. First there was
the silence of Jesus. How hard it is to carry on praying to God
when he seems to be ignoring us, and is deaf to our prayers!
But the woman passed through that barrier. Then she had the
disciples to contend with when they begged Jesus to send her
away because she had become a problem to them. Then she
had to put up with the seeming insults from Jesus himself.
Luther called this 'the method and trick of wrestling with
God'.[26] When we look at the wider canvas of Jesus' ministry
of healing we can see three hindrances which were overcome
by faith in ascending order. First the paralysed man who was
let down by his friends through the roof. That was a physical
hindrance. With blind Bartimaeus it was his fellow men who
tried to stop him. But with this woman it was Christ himself
who made things difficult for her. The commendation of Jesus
– 'great is your faith' – was truly deserved.

8.   The woman with the bent back
    Lk 13:10–17

In this story the woman's condition is specified as satanic.
Jesus describes her as a woman 'whom Satan bound for
eighteen years' (v.16). This is not a case of deliverance in the
sense of an evil spirit being cast out. But it is a striking

example of Satan directly intervening to cause physical disability. In this case there is no rebuking of Satan or taking authority over his power. Instead there is a straight forward laying-on of hands.

Although this story gives us further helpful insights into Jesus' healing ministry, and further proof that satanic influence does need to be taken seriously in that ministry, the main purpose for which it is recorded is because it provides evidence of the mounting confrontation between Jesus and the religious establishment. The healing had taken place in a synagogue on the sabbath and the ruler of the synagogue was much displeased. He expressed this in a speech to the congregation. Jesus' reply was to draw attention to the hypocrisy whereby the watering of livestock on the sabbath was allowed, although involving considerable physical effort, whereas the compassionate ministry to the sick, in this case a woman who had suffered greatly for eighteen years, was forbidden, even though it required no physical effort whatsoever.

It is possible that this was a psychosomatic problem. It has been suggested that the woman may have been an hysteric. No one can know for certain. What we do know is that she had suffered for a long time, that no one had been able to help her until she met Jesus and he had prayed for her, and that Satan had been the direct cause of the illness. This is what is presented to us, and it provides substantial encouragement since we have the same authority today to loose those whom Satan has bound. The need for careful discernment (which is in itself a gift of the Holy Spirit) is clear. We need to know what really lies behind every kind of sickness.

Another interesting aspect of this case is that Jesus takes the initiative, whereas on other occasions it is the other way round. This yet again highlights the responsibility we have in discerning what we should do. Should we wait for people to come for healing or should we, as in this case, take the initiative ourselves? There can be no hard and fast rule. As in every other aspect of this ministry we need to be guided by the Holy Spirit, as Jesus so clearly was.

This case is a happy hunting ground for those who see psychological clues everywhere in the New Testament. Micklem examines it closely along these lines, while Fenner sees it as a case of scoliosis hysteria.[27] Loos calls it 'mental impotence'.[28] But it is not the purpose of this book to speculate along these lines.

It is interesting that Jesus here calls the woman a 'daughter of Abraham', just as later on he is to call Zacchaeus a 'son of Abraham' (Lk 19:9). It shows Jesus' Jewish pride. It is also an example of the way Jesus used words and gestures to affirm and encourage people, especially those who were down-trodden, as the Jews of his day so often were. Zacchaeus would have suffered humiliation not only from the Romans, who treated the Jews with disdain, but also from his fellow countrymen who regarded him as a traitor. It is also likely that this woman had been mistreated and humiliated because of her physical weakness and had been the butt of many hurtful comments and jokes. The disabled in those days were seldom treated with the dignity and care they are today.

Here too we see Jesus restoring a woman to human whole-ness. Man, unlike the animal creation, was created erect. As we say today, he 'stands tall'. The Greek word for man (*anthropos*) has a derivation which means 'upward looking', as if that is our human destiny. Augustine draws attention to the *sursum corda*, the call in the Eucharist to 'lift up your hearts'.[29] He writes 'for with erect stature man looks for the hope laid up for him in heaven . . .' This is in contrast with those who are forever looking at the ground. Frederich Langbridge once wrote:

> Two men look out through the same bars:
> One sees the mud, and one the stars.

Satan can bend us physically, as he did in this woman's case. But he also frequently attempts, and sometimes succeeds, in bending us spiritually so that our gaze is directed downwards rather than upwards, so that we become overwhelmingly mean and materialistic. We need to realise our true humanity, which is to stand spiritually as well as physically erect. In this story it was surely the ruler of the synagogue who was suffering from curvature of the soul. What sort of a God can he have worshipped who allows the loosing of an animal who has been bound only for a few hours and forbids the loosing of a woman, one of God's own people, who has been bound for eighteen years?

Calvin exhorted his readers to war against those forces which have conspired together to effect man's ruin. Jesus Christ has placed in the hands of the church the keys of the kingdom (Mt 16:19). One of these keys will set men and women free from the power and authority of Satan. We need to use this key wisely but resolutely. It will not fit every lock. But the locks it does fit will spring open at the name of Jesus Christ. The authority Jesus had to deliver people from satanic powers has been bequeathed to the church. It may be used wherever and whenever it is appropriate.

Chapter
4

Your Sins Are Forgiven

> The terms for 'salvation' in many languages are derived
> from roots like salvus, saos, whole, heil, which all
> designate health, the opposite of disintegration and
> disruption. Salvation is healing in the ultimate sense.
> Paul Tillich

We have just seen that the acceptance of the reality of satanic
powers is largely discounted in our churches. Equally we find
less acceptance of human responsibility for sin. This is
reflected in the decline of the confessional in churches like the
Roman Catholic where it is practised. 'Sin' is regarded by
many as an ugly word which only nurtures guilt; and society at
large, like Lady Macbeth, is forever washing its hands to rid
itself of the guilt which psychologists treat largely as a disease
from which we only need to be healed.

The situation has not been helped by Protestant and
evangelical legalism which have at times heaped guilt on
people and given them little chance of ever breaking free
from its all-embracing grasp. For some it can be almost the
unpardonable sin not to feel guilty, and 'crying for mercy'
can be an occupational disease for such people. Maybe we
need help from the Eastern Church which views sin almost as
another word for humanity. This makes it rather easier to
understand, and delivers us from the guilt-ridden overtones
which can cause so much psychological damage to sensitive
people.

Jesus came to this planet not only to overpower Satan but
also to restore the damage caused by human sin since the fall.
His name itself reveals this purpose – 'you shall call his name

Jesus, for he will save his people from their sins' (Mt 1:21). When Jesus began to minister, his message was clear and simple – 'The time is fulfilled, and the kingdom of God is at hand; repent and believe in the gospel' (Mk 1:15). Repentance always had a place in the ministry of Jesus Christ. He called everyone to acknowledge and turn from their sins. In the Bible sin is always personal never institutional. It may be individual or corporate; but no person can hide behind a shadowy institution and point an accusing finger at 'it'. 'It' does not sin, only human beings sin, and they have shown remarkable aptitudes in doing just that.

The subject of this book is not Jesus' salvation but his healings. But a simple and cursory examination of the New Testament shows that there are links and associations between salvation and health as well as between sin and sickness which make it difficult to study the one without the other. It would seem from the evidence of the New Testament, and what we know from other Jewish sources of the time, that Jesus' Jewish contemporaries did see an identification between sickness and sin. Whenever anyone was sick the question was invariably asked, 'What has this person done wrong to be in this condition?' It is an equation which has lingered on in the church and has at times caused widespread injustice and spiritual harm.

One of the clearest examples of this can be found in the Order for the Visitation of the Sick in the old Anglican Prayer Book. The implications of this service are that sickness is normally God's chastisement for human sin. No wonder false guilt has been nurtured in sick people causing unnecessary suffering. It is well known that the antagonism of the church to the rise of the medical profession and the development of medical science in the Middle Ages was largely based on the view that sickness was sent by God and, therefore, healing a person was interfering with that will. Sometimes sickness was regarded as a punishment for sins committed; sometimes it was sent as a means of purging or refining the person.

Jesus was at pains to show that identification between the

practice of sin and the experience of sickness could not always be established. The key was discernment. In at least two cases, as we shall see, Jesus discerned that there was such a connection and that sin needed to be confessed and renounced before the person could be healed. The exact nature of that connection is not revealed. On the other hand John records for us another case in which Jesus indicated that human sin had nothing to do with the situation of the patient at all. The importance of the gifts of the Holy Spirit is clearly demonstrated in these stories. Because Jesus knew what was in each person, he was able to minister according to that knowledge; in one case to minister forgiveness and absolution, because he knew that sin was involved in the sickness, and in the other case to make it plain that the man was not sick because of his sin, and so sin was irrelevant.

We shall, therefore, examine these two stories side by side to see both aspects. The leprosy stories (of which there are two in the gospels) have been chosen for another reason. Whether leprosy in the Bible is the same disease as modern leprosy is debatable. We shall have to look at that also. But it is the theological interpretation of leprosy which is more important and perhaps even more controversial. I have included the leprosy healings because they really belong to this section. Actually the word 'healing' is never directly applied to them in the gospels, it is always the word 'cleansing'. At least, therefore, for the gospel writers, leprosy was in a different category. And the fact that the word 'cleansing' is used implies that they regarded the disease as having a link with human sinfulness. But we need to go deeper into this. Here then are the four cases we shall be examining:

1. The man let down through the roof (Mt 9:1–8; Mk 2:1–12; Lk 5:17–26).
2. The man born blind (Jn 9:1–41).
3. The one leper (Mt 8:1–4; Mk 1:40–45; Lk 5:12–16).
4. The ten lepers (Lk 17:11–19).

1. The man let down through the roof
Mt 9:1–8; Mk 2:1–12; Lk 5:17–26

This is one of the most remembered of the healings of Jesus because it shows the ingeniousness of faith. The friends who let the paralysed man down through the roof may have been jumping the line; they were also interrupting the flow of Jesus' teaching. Never mind. Jesus was never offended by interruptions when they were demonstrations of faith and confidence in him. Perhaps Peter, whose house it may have been, remembered this incident when preaching in the home of Cornelius. His talk was also dramatically interrupted when his audience was baptised in the Holy Spirit and spoke in tongues (Acts 10). Someone has written 'love will creep but faith will climb where it cannot go'.

There are some textual problems in the account of the man let through the roof, but this is a matter for the commentaries not for us. Luke does have an important addition, the words, 'and the power of the Lord was with him to heal' (5:17). His addition would indicate that the power and authority that Jesus had was not like a water supply which could be turned on and off at will. There was more to it than that. There were occasions when the power was especially present and other occasions when, presumably, it was not. Sometimes this was due to the presence of unbelief or direct antagonism to his ministry. At other times there was no particular reason for the ebb and flow of healing grace. Those who are involved in a Christian healing ministry today would agree that the same happens in their experience. Sometimes the power is there and sometimes it isn't and there is often no clear explanation for such variation.

My own experience over many years is that a good climate of faith is essential. When one is amongst those who question the lordship of Jesus or faith in his power to heal, nothing much will happen. A spirit of expectation is all important.

A traditional interpretation, dating back at least to Jerome and Ambrose, is that when we read Jesus 'saw their faith' (Lk 5:20) it refers to the men (Mark tells us there were four of

them) who carried the paralysed man to the house and let him
down through the roof. Chrysostom deferred and believed
'their faith' included that of the sick man. We can't be sure; all
we do know is that it certainly included the four who carried
the man and brought him so ingeniously to the feet of Jesus
Christ. We must assume that the sick person was at least
cooperative. Personally I believe the sick man planned the
whole operation, although I have no proof of that. Bengel
comments 'faith penetrates through all obstacles to come to
Christ'.[1] Although the sovereignty of God can be seen in the
statement that the power of God was 'present to heal', there is
an even clearer indication of free will and human activity in
the manner in which this man came to Jesus. It is good also to
notice that Jesus *saw* their faith. Faith needs at times to be
public and visible, seen by everyone.

The gospel writers often selected the healing stories which
involved conflict between Jesus and the religious establishment of his day. The issue of the sabbath, and what could and
could not be done on it, is one example. Here the issue is even
more fundamental. Jesus claimed to forgive sins, something
which the Jews believed only God could do. So Jesus was
accused of blasphemy. It was a controversy which eventually
led to his crucifixion. This healing was a demonstration of
Jesus' power, which others including his disciples had, but it
was also visible proof that Jesus had the authority, which only
God possessed, to forgive sins. The reader is left to draw the
obvious conclusions.

The reason I've included this healing in the present section
is because it shows a link between human sin and sickness. We
are not told what this man's sin was. Jesus would have been
too sensitive to have publicly revealed it anyway. He would
have known it through the gift of the word of knowledge and
the spiritual discernment which always characterised his
ministry. The Holy Spirit would have revealed it to him. As
far as the question Jesus asks his opponents (whether it is
easier to forgive sins or to heal the sick), it is much easier to
pronounce the forgiveness of sins (an invisible blessing) than
to heal the sick (which is visible). However, the fact that Jesus

indicates that the healing of the paralysed man is proof that he did have authority to forgive sins is most significant. One would have expected him to have prefaced the call to be healed with the words 'that you may know the Son of Man has authority on earth to heal the sick'. The fact that he says 'to forgive sin' would indicate that there was in this case a direct link between the declaration of forgiveness and the healing of the paralysed man, for the healing was the proof that the forgiveness had been effective. It would also indicate that the healing process could not begin until the man had been forgiven.

Sometimes in the healing stories forgiveness follows the outward healing, as in the case of the thankful Samaritan (Lk 17:19) and the impotent man (Jn 5:14), stories which we shall be looking at in a moment. But here forgiveness of sins comes first, then healing. The epistle of James gives us an interesting parallel. In James 5:14–16 the link between healing and forgiveness of sins is firmly established. What is interesting is that the passage supports what we have already seen in the gospels, namely that forgiveness sometimes has to precede healing and sometimes to follow it. In v. 15, for instance, healing appears to precede forgiveness, whereas in v. 16 confession of sins precedes healing and seems to be a condition of it.

We also need to notice in this story the part that words of authority play. Both the words of absolution of sins and the summons to healing, 'rise, take up your bed and go home' (v. 24), are declaratory. They are declaring what is happening not expressing the desire for it to happen. There is the world of difference between declaration and desire. We can pray, expressing our desires and hoping that what we ask for we shall in due course receive. That is not what Jesus is doing here. He is not praying but *declaring*. His words of authority actually bring what he says to pass. He is not saying 'I hope you will be forgiven'; he is saying 'you are forgiven'. He is not saying, 'I hope you will be healed'; he is saying 'you are healed'. Actually Jesus does not pray for this man to be healed. All he does is to tell him to do what he had to do after being healed – 'get up and take your stretcher home with you'. In other words he assumes the man is healed and declares it to be a fact by issuing practical instructions as to the next steps he needs to take.

This is an example of the fact that Jesus did not normally pray for the sick as such. He declared them healed and whole. It was his word that counted. Human touch is sometimes important, and Jesus was ready to make it a little easier for the sick person to respond to the word which he spoke. But it was the word, not the touch, that healed.

No one involved in Christian healing can avoid the fact that human sin does play some part in disease and sickness. Obviously we need to avoid (as Jesus did) the equation that much sickness equals much sin. Sometimes a person is more sinned against than guilty of their own sins. Nevertheless forgiveness will often play an important part in the healing process. Even if there are times when we do not need to be forgiven ourselves, we are bound to need to forgive others; and a spirit of unforgiveness can be a potent fact in hindering the healing power of Christ.

2. The man born blind
   Jn 9:1–41

This story begins in John 7. Jesus probably only visited Jerusalem once between his baptism by John and the final week of his earthly life. We are not in the least surprised that his time there was overshadowed by controversy and confrontation with his enemies, who were already plotting to do away with him. All through this visit he was disputing with those people, particularly the Pharisees. The climax comes in John 8:59 when they took up stones to throw at him, an attack from which Jesus chose to escape.

While escaping from the attempt on his life he saw this man, whose name we don't know, who had been blind from birth. His disciples raised the controversial question of the relationship between sin and sickness, inferring in the question that they accepted the commonly held belief of those days that disabilities, even if incurred from birth, were the judgement of God on human sin. The disciples seem to have assumed that the only possible explanation as to why this man was blind from birth was his own sin or the sin of his parents (v. 2).

One can understand the disciples thinking it was parental sin which affected the foetus in some way or other. But it is hard to know why they thought it was the sin of the man himself, which must have been pre-natal to have caused the blindness. Perhaps it was because the Jews believed that the human foetus could sin before birth; the struggle between the twins Jacob and Esau had been used as evidence of this.

Other views have been suggested. But why should we expect the disciples to have always been rational when they spoke, especially in circumstances of stress such as on this occasion? It would seem clear that the link between sin and sickness was dominant in their minds, but they would probably not have rationally worked out the difficult moral and personal questions such a view inevitably raises. That sin and suffering do have a connection is true; but the way in which we apply it to each personal situation needs discernment.

Jesus' reply, 'It was not that this man sinned, or his parents' (v. 3), does not imply that they had never sinned. What he is saying is that the blindness of this man was not due to his parents' sin. In a general sense all sickness is due to sin since it is not part of God's original purposes for his creatures. But we must not jump from that general statement and apply it specifically to individuals and see personal sin as *always* being the cause of sickness. Sometimes it is, but here Jesus is correcting the judgemental attitudes of the disciples, which were a reflection of the views of many in those days. God was punishing these people, so the argument went, one must not, therefore, interfere. It was a convenient way of neglecting the sick and disabled.

However, Jesus saw it all in a different light. This man was born blind, 'that the works of God might be made manifest in him' (v. 3). Jesus was about to heal him for that very purpose.

Healing which comes from God does manifest the divine
grace and glory, and, therefore, is a wholly beneficial ministry, which is to be sought and practised by the whole church.
But there are many people born with disabilities, such as
blindness, who are not going to be healed in this life. For them
the works of God can still be manifested in and through their
disability. It is for us to discover the will of God in each
instance, and then pray accordingly. But whether the people
we pray for are healed or not – and God will show us who to
pray for – they can always live to God's glory, and do the
works of God in spite of their human weaknesses. Thus Jesus
shifted the question which the disciples raised from the cause
of sickness (sin) to the purpose of it (the glory of God). It is
important that we never lose sight of this goal.

We can also see in this story the importance that Jesus
attached to signs and means. Sometimes it was a matter of
'blind faith'. But here is an example of Jesus asking a sick
person to do something, 'Go, wash in the pool of Siloam', and
Jesus doing something himself, spitting on the ground and
making clay from it to anoint the man's eyes (vv. 6–7). From
the church fathers onwards some have seen special significance in the details given. Irenaeus for example compares
Genesis 2:7 with this action of Jesus, and suggests that the
blind man received new eyes made by the clay.[2] Modern
commentators take a much more practical line. They see
nothing medicinal in what Jesus did, but see Jesus' aim as
pedagogic and psychological (e.g. Jeremias).[3] It was a means
of arousing faith. The medical profession has long seen the
importance of the relationship between doctor and patient,
and the need for the patient to have confidence in the doctor.
Out of that confident relationship an atmosphere is created
which is in itself therapeutic. Jesus was no doubt developing
just such a relationship, and the man's faith was being
nurtured by it. It would seem that the man was not helped
until he had carried out Jesus' instructions. It was only after
he had washed in the pool of Siloam that he 'came back
seeing' (v. 7).

Again there are those who see symbolism in the man

washing in the pool. Keulers writes 'Obviously John thought of baptism; for Jesus brings about the healing through the water of the pool.'[4] This is reading too much into the story. If you emphasise symbolism you can distort the main message of this story, which is about the power of God's healing, not the water of the pool. Going to the pool helped this man's faith. But the main factor was not the water, or the clay for that matter, but the work of Jesus Christ and this man's faith in him. It was a work of God not a work of nature; but the creator of all nature used clay and water on this occasion to stimulate faith and confidence so that this powerful miracle of healing could take place.

Once again we see sin in the religious leaders, who were more concerned about the sabbath laws than that this man was healed. 'This man is not from God, for he does not keep the sabbath', some of the Pharisees said (v. 16). In the gospels we are constantly shown that the healing ministry of Jesus did not take place in a vacuum. Usually there was a background of antagonism to the kind of radical reformation which Jesus clearly believed to be necessary, and which he fearlessly proclaimed. The healing ministry today can create similar tensions and presents painful challenges to establishments more concerned with law than life, with perpetuating traditions than moving freely in the Spirit. For Jesus people mattered more than things, and he was crucified for it.

Leprosy – ancient and modern

Leprosy has always had a stigma attached to it, and those who have contracted the disease have almost universally been ostracised by society. In the Far East leprosy has been diagnosed as a punishment for sexual misdemeanour. In India a belief is widely held that it is the punishment of the gods for sins in a previous existence. Muslims regard it as the will of God and, therefore, it has to be accepted without complaint. Amongst animists it is regarded as the displeasure of the spirits. In many parts of the world the fears and taboos associated with the disease make treatment difficult. The early symptoms are never easy to discover, and the stigmas attached to it, mean that the disease is seldom diagnosed in its early stages. Society's distaste and horror of it mean that rehabilitation after treatment is also difficult. Only rarely in primitive societies are lepers allowed back into the community even though it is well known that the disease is not very contagious.

The word 'leprosy' is a translation of the Hebrew word *sara'at* which is used in all the relevant Old Testament texts. It is very likely that the primary root of this word means 'collapse' or 'strike', and thus came to mean 'stricken of God'. It would seem from the texts that the disease was disfiguring and affected any surface, including the walls of a house (see Leviticus chapter 13 and 14). Since there are obviously important links between leprosy in the Old and New Testaments, we need to look closely at what the Old Testament says about leprosy and leave on one side medical questions, particularly those relating to the modern understanding of the disease.

Looking at the Old Testament references to 'leprosy' we become immediately aware that the law of Moses treated aliens and foreign visitors differently from the Israelites themselves. Strangers and foreigners were exempt from laws relating to leprosy. Since we know that modern leprosy and most other forms of skin disease are not very contagious, this should not surprise us. Thus Naaman, the commander-in-chief of the Syrian army, was able to carry on his leadership role and mix with society although he was a leper (2 Kings 5:1). If leprosy was contagious it is difficult to see how the Levitical priests could have safely examined those suffering from the disease, and, indeed, how in 2 Kings 8:5, Gehazi could have talked face to face with the king of apostate Israel. Had he been an Israelite it would have been impossible. It seems that the strict laws relating to leprosy had a religious or spiritual reason behind them rather than a strictly sanitary one.

Archbishop Trench and others have suggested that God

took one sickness (out of many) to demonstrate the meaning of evil and its effects on individuals as well as society at large.[5] Leprosy for the Jews was nothing short of a living death. According to Numbers 12:12 Miriam was 'as one dead, of whom the flesh is half consumed . . .' For the Jews it was a symbol and parable of the effect of human sin in a person's life. Sin separates us from God and from one another. So does leprosy. Sin slowly rots away human life. So does leprosy. Sin is at first not easy to diagnose; it works silently and secretly. So does leprosy. Sin disfigures and distorts. So does leprosy. Sin paralyses and removes feeling and sensitivity. So does leprosy. Sin ultimately causes death. So does leprosy. It would be difficult looking at the whole range of human diseases to find a single one which more graphically describes human sinfulness than leprosy. The leper is commanded by the law to 'look the part'. His clothes are to be torn, his hair hang loose and he is to cry wherever he goes, 'Unclean, unclean' (Lev 13:45). Sin also leads us into loneliness and isolation. It separates us from people. The leper was commanded to live alone in a place outside the camp of Israel (Lev 13:46).

The same imagery can be found in other places in the Old Testament. Thus in David's confession in Psalm 51 he cries, 'Purge me with hyssop, and I shall be clean; wash me, and I shall be whiter than snow' (v. 7). Here he sees himself as a spiritual leper. In Isaiah 53:4 the suffering servant is described as 'smitten by God', which again takes us to the roots of the word 'leprosy' in Hebrew. In the Vulgate Jerome translates the word *leprosus*, which has added weight to an old tradition that Jesus was leprous when he hung on the cross.

The link between leprosy and sin is well established in the Old Testament; but it is important to stress the symbolic nature of this. We are not to conclude, even in the earliest stages of development in the Old Testament, that lepers were more sinful than their fellows. However there are three instances, namely those of Miriam, Gehazi and Uzziah, when leprosy is stated to be a punishment for actual and specific sins (Num 12; 2 Kings 5 and 2 Chron 26).

Jesus and the lepers

The texts of the New Testament indicate that society's attitude to lepers had hardened even further by the time of Jesus. In the excessively judgemental and legalistic atmosphere of his day we can be certain that the laws relating to leprosy were applied even more strictly. It is possible that there existed a more direct equation between sin and this particular sickness, so that leprosy was popularly regarded as the punishment of God meted out for particularly heinous personal sins. What had been in the Old Testament an illustration of the relationship between God and man marred by human sin, was now regarded as an example of suffering because of personal sin.

How then did Jesus deal with this situation? In the first instance he went along with it, and this comes out in two main respects. Firstly he abided by the law and told the lepers he ministered to, 'go and show yourselves to the priest' (Lk 5:14; 17:14). But secondly, it is said of his ministry to them that he 'cleansed' rather than 'healed' them. The one exception to this is the statement in Luke 17:15 that one of the ten lepers was 'healed'. However this leper was not Jewish but a Samaritan. When Jesus commissioned the twelve, according to Matthew's gospel, he told them to 'Heal the sick . . . cleanse lepers . . .' (10:8). The gospels are tacitly assuming that there is a distinction between the ministry to the sick and to lepers, and that lepers needed to be cleansed. This comes out too in Jesus' instructions to the one leper in Luke 5 to 'make an offering for your cleansing, as Moses commanded, for a proof to the people' (v. 14).

But there is a second feature in the ministry of Jesus in which he does not identify with or in the least accommodate himself to the views of his contemporaries. Jesus shows a compassion towards lepers which laid the foundation for the gradual removal of the stigma which had been attached to them. Jesus undermined and ultimately demolished the popular equation that sickness was the result of sin, and, therefore, those with the worst forms of disease (particularly leprosy) were the greatest of sinners. It seems that Jesus reserved some of his greatest demonstrations of compassion for those who were outcasts of society, not least lepers. In Luke 5:13 we are told that Jesus did something that was quite unheard of, 'he stretched out his hand, and *touched*' the leper. *No one touched lepers*. And one of Jesus' friends was called Simon the *leper* (Mt 26:6; Mk 14:3). Whether he was one whom Jesus had 'cleansed' or whether Jesus was deliberately breaking one of the Jewish taboos we don't know. All we know is that this man was one of the Bethany circle of friends.

Leprosy today

Leprosy is a widespread disease, according to figures from the World Health Organization. It is still growing in spite of drugs and a network of Christian and secular health organisations throughout the world. It has nearly doubled in the last sixteen years, and a billion people are at risk. In some areas it is out of control and increasingly resistant to drugs. Today, many question whether modern leprosy can be equated with the Hebrew word *sara'at*, normally translated 'leprosy'. There are a number of reasons given for this. The first is that modern leprosy is generally regarded as incurable, whereas in both the Old and New Testaments provision is made for leprous patients to be declared 'cleansed' or healed by the Levitical priests. Secondly, the clinical features described in Leviticus to enable the priest to make a positive diagnosis of *sara'at* are not applicable to true leprosy. For example, whiteness of the hair (leucotrichia) does not occur in leprosy. Stanley G. Browne, a Christian leprologist, has done an exhaustive study of the various symptoms described in Leviticus and has concluded that they are not describing leprosy as we know it today. According to him they may be descriptive of what we call psoriasis or prurigo or scurf. Since leprosy does affect the bones of patients it is possible to examine skeletons and mummies for traces of the disease. None have yet been found

and the earliest definite description of the disease dates from
India around 600 BC.

It has been suggested that the disease was relayed to the
western world, including Palestine, by the army of Alexander
the Great returning from India in 327–326 BC. All this has a
degree of speculation about it. It is also claimed that what we
call leprosy, which was first clinically defined as the organism
mycobacterium leprae by Hansen in 1874, was unknown in the
Old Testament period, and *sara'at* covered a wider range of
skin diseases. However it is conjectured that this organism
was eventually brought to the west and emerged in Palestine
as well as generally elsewhere. It was simply bracketed with
all the other skin diseases covered by the word *sara'at*.

We need, however, to challenge some of these assumptions. For instance, it is not true that all leprosy is incurable.
Some forms are, others are not. And if biblical leprosy, as is
sometimes alleged, is only a mixture of scurf, psoriasis and
prurigo, then it makes nonsense of the statements that are
made in the Old Testament which regard it as something
much more radical and serious. For example, how could it
seriously be singled out to be 'a living death' if that was all it
was? It is more likely that the term 'leprosy' in the Old and
New Testaments included what we understand by leprosy,
and that those whom Jesus healed had the kind of leprosy
which we know today. If this is so, then the healings were truly
remarkable, almost certainly unique for those days. Thus
Jesus Christ, who had come to cleanse the world of the
'leprosy' of sin, healed lepers as a sign of that much greater
and universal work of grace. He had compassion and power to
'cleanse' some of the lepers of Palestine as a sign of the
coming total victory over human sin at Calvary.

3. The one leper
   Mt 8:1–4; Mk 1:40–45; Lk 5:12–16

Anyone who has been present and seen a person healed of
leprosy will tell you what a dramatic event it is. We should not

be the least surprised at the results which followed when Jesus healed this man, no wonder 'great multitudes gathered to hear and to be healed of their infirmities' (Lk 5:15). It is to be expected that Jesus tried to keep this man from telling people what had happened. Jesus knew it would hamper his wider ministry, and he was right. However we should not be too hard on the man. How difficult it must have been to keep quiet about such a remarkable healing! Luke, as one would expect from a doctor, gives us one extra medical detail. This man was apparently 'full of leprosy' (v. 12), which would mean the advanced stages of the disease.

If this was what we know today as leprosy, then this man had remarkable faith. The gospels say it was an instant healing. Mark uses a strong word for Jesus' instructions to this man. Jesus 'banished him', rather like he did the demons. He 'sent him away' and 'sternly charged him' (Mk 1:43). Perhaps Jesus was anxious that he should go quickly to the priest before the news got there first as to what had happened. A prejudiced priest might then have been reluctant to declare this man 'clean'. It would have been natural for the man to hang around, perhaps wanting to know more about Jesus. It was characteristic of the compassion and wisdom of Jesus that he saw the need for this man to get clearance quickly. It shows that Jesus Christ was just as concerned about after-care or 'follow-up' as he was about healing people.

Jesus also speaks of the need to go to the priest 'for a proof to them' (Mk 1:44 mg). It is not clear exactly what the proof was, nor whether this was for the sake of the priest or the people. Either Jesus was concerned to respect and obey the law, or what he had done was proof of his messiahship. It could also have been a testimony against (the Greek can be translated this way) his enemies in the religious establishment. It would force the hands of the priests; they would have to accept this miracle and, therefore, to face up to his claims to be the Messiah.

But this is not in keeping with Jesus' normal low-profile approach. He usually wanted to avoid both open confrontation with his enemies amongst the religious leaders, and also being made into a famous and popular figure by the crowds. He never made the mistake of entrusting himself to fickle crowds or mobs, and he spent more time avoiding his enemies than facing them. He knew that hour was coming; but it hadn't arrived yet, and the timing would be his not theirs. For the time being he wanted to avoid any misunderstandings which might arise, particularly any relating to the law, as much as possible. To be dubbed a law-breaker was a reputation he was not keen to have. Sometimes Jesus' ministry was hampered more by his own success than the opposition of his enemies. Hence his stern command to this man to obey the law.

4. The ten lepers
   Lk 17:11–19

This incident, recorded only by Luke, comes much later in Jesus' ministry. Indeed it took place on his final journey to Jerusalem somewhere between Samaria and Galilee. It is not surprising that Luke records this story; Luke shows particular interest in Jesus' ministry to the poor and the underprivileged. There is an interesting twist to this story, for we are told that the ten lepers, as they left Jesus, were *cleansed*, but the one leper who came back to return thanks was *healed* (v. 15). This is further underlined by the words of Jesus to the one who returned, 'Rise and go your way; your faith has made you well' (v. 19). The removal of leprosy is one thing, healing and wholeness is something else. The removal of disease and sickness, and being made whole in the full sense of that word, are different. The Samaritan who returned to give thanks was a candidate for wholeness, the others were not.

This story underlines something else which is important. The gospel writers are not interested, generally speaking, in healings for their own sake or on their own. They are usually mentioned in connection with another issue. In this case it is a racial issue, the Jewish-Samaritan controversy. On other occasions it is conflict with the law, particularly relating to the sabbath. Practically every miracle of Jesus accompanies additional events, and they are seen in relationship to the favourable or unfavourable reactions of the spectators. The enthusiastic support of the crowds is in marked contrast to the malevolence of the Pharisees. This is the backcloth to all that Jesus did from his baptism in the Jordan to his greater baptism at Calvary. Healings and miracles never happen in a vacuum. They demand a response. For those with eyes to see and ears to hear they are pointers to principles and blessings which are more important than the events themselves. For others they are to be either dismissed out of hand or strenuously opposed.

Jesus sets sinners free. That message is one that comes loud and clear throughout the Bible. But the healings of Jesus shed fresh and stronger light on the nature of sin itself. The understanding of personal ethics had become warped in his day, and judgement was often passed on those to whom the Lord showed mercy. One of the greatest temptations of the religious is to pass judgement on others through the exalting of the letter of the law and a strange blindness to its spirit. Thus the sick, particularly lepers, were seen as being punished for their sins. Jesus came to liberate us from that dogmatism which always equates sickness and personal sin. The healing of lepers by Jesus went a long way towards removing the stigma society in those days placed on them.

How better to end this chapter than with a modern example of a healing from leprosy in the Third World which reminds one immediately of Jesus' healing of lepers in the first century? I am grateful to the Anglican Bishop of Morogoro (Dr Gresford Chitemo) for the details of this healing. The man's name is Emmanuel Hamis, and he was a Moslem. After he had contracted leprosy he left his village of Matombo in Morogoro and went to Dar-es-Salaam. He got a job, but when his leprosy got worse he reported to a mission hospital in Dar-es-Salaam and stayed for a while in the leprosy section. However, after a time he discharged himself and went into the city and began a criminal life, stealing, getting drunk and taking drugs. He was arrested and sent to prison.

After his release his condition got much worse and his friends deserted him. He could no longer help himself, so he decided to return home. His step-mother abused him, so that he left home again and returned to Dar-es-Salaam. His whole body became very swollen, his fingers were eaten away. He had a large hole in the palm of his hands, a wound on his thigh and sores all over his body. So he decided to return to the hospital. Being penniless he went to an old friend called Jonas, who welcomed him and gave him food. The leper then asked for some money and Jonas gave him it. The leper said, 'thank you'. 'Don't say "thank you",' said Jonas, 'say "thank you Jesus".' They then began to talk about Jesus. Jonas told him that the Jesus who had given him the money could also heal him.

Emmanuel agreed to go to a prayer group so that they might minister to him. They told him to say 'thank you Jesus' while they prayed for him. As they were praising God together the man began to vomit violently. He returned to his room and slept soundly for the first time for many years. In the morning he gathered together all his medicines and his marijuana, put them in a big parcel, and then carried them to the garbage dump. He waited to see the city council truck remove it. Returning to his room he slept until the evening, when he went to the meeting. They prayed for him again and he was healed. As a result of his healing all his body skin came off like a snake when it sheds its own skin. All the scars left by the big sores and wounds could still be seen.

Emmanuel's first concern was to share this with his Moslem friends. His father became a Christian, and two churches were formed in his village. Healing is a sign to bring people to Christ, and this is especially true amongst Moslems who do not believe in divine healing.

This is one of many examples one could give of healings drawing men and women to faith in the Lord Jesus Christ today. 'Signs and wonders' always increase evangelistic success and contribute significantly to the spreading of the gospel everywhere.

Chapter
5

The Last Enemy Is Destroyed

Christianity is a religion of miracle, and the miracle of
Christ's Resurrection is the living centre and object of
Christian Faith.

Alan Richardson

It is Paul in 1 Corinthians 15:26 who describes death as 'the
last enemy'. Christ destroys it. We have been seeing the role
of Jesus as 'liberator': the most far-reaching and dramatic
liberation of all is the one he secured over death. For a short
time it seemed that death had won. The voice of the Son of
God was silent; his heart was no longer beating; his arms and
legs, for several hours cruelly nailed to a wooden cross, were
motionless. The disciples, their minds filled with questions
not faith, forgot the words Jesus had spoken to them about his
rising on the third day. Then one by one their mourning was
turned into joy as the message passed from mouth to mouth,
'the Lord is risen'.

The resurrection of Jesus Christ from the dead lies at the
heart of the Christian message. Remove it, and Christianity
simply becomes another philosophy, albeit an extremely
good one, the story of a remarkable man with divine qualities
rather than God's only begotten Son, who through his own
death destroyed death and brought 'life and immortality' to
light through his resurrection (2 Tim 1:10). If this is indeed the
central truth of Christianity it should not surprise us that Jesus
raised people from the dead. The one who came to liberate
the whole of mankind from the finality of death gave notice
of his far-reaching purposes and the full implications of them,
by raising at least three people from the condition of death.

But Jesus did not introduce 'raising the dead', nor were the examples given in the gospels novelties. The fact that Lazarus was raised from the dead several days after he had died has no precedence so far as we know in human history, but the fact that he was raised was no new thing. The Old Testament records that the feat was done by Elijah and Elisha (1 Kings 17:17–24; 2 Kings 4:18–37). There is also a reference to the bones of Elisha being used to raise the dead (2 Kings 13:20, 21). So Jesus was not doing anything particularly new.

There are also unsubstantiated legends in Jewish tradition. There is an amusing story about Rabbi Ze'ira, who was murdered by a man called Rabbah, who was drunk during the feast of Purim. The next day he begged for mercy and brought him back to life. The following year Rabbah suggested they again celebrated Purim together. Ze'ira's response was, 'a miracle does not happen every hour!' He clearly did not fancy his chances a second time!

The Christian apocryphal literature is full of examples, including Paul's raising of Patrochus, Nero's cupbearer, who had fallen out of a top-storey window. John is also credited with several raisings. Irenaeus mentioned the raisings of Jesus and the apostles, and went on to point out that those who had been raised from the dead 'continued to live among us for many years'. No doubt some of the apocryphal stories may be myths. But the accounts are so varied it is likely that some were genuine, and Irenaeus knew this and may have personally known some of the people concerned.

Again we should not be surprised at the reaction of people to these stories. The enemies of Jesus were full of indignation and began to draw up their plans to kill him (John 11:53). For them it was the last straw. Opposition to Jesus' teaching and actions, particularly the healings, reached a climax. We find a similar response from modern critics of the miraculous. Many modern liberal scholars deny the truth of these stories and relegate them to the category of myths. The same is true of modern accounts of the raising of the dead which are often treated with scepticism or explained away. It is a crunch issue, for raising the dead cannot be explained away psychologically. It either happens or it doesn't. Is Jesus the Lord over death as well as life? If he is the Lord of both, then why shouldn't he restore to life those who have been declared clinically dead? The healings of Jesus reach their climax in these stories, particularly the raising of Lazarus in John 11; but the stories are only the overture to the main work of God's power and grace, the resurrection of Jesus himself by the Father through the power of the Holy Spirit.

In the gospels there are three stories of Jesus raising people from the dead:

1. The young daughter of Jairus (Mt 9:18–26; Mk 5:22–43; Lk 8:41–56).
2. The young son of the widow of Nain (Lk 7:11–17).
3. Jesus' friend Lazarus (Jn 11:1–44).

1. The young daughter of Jairus
   Mt 9:18–26; Mk 5:22–43; Lk 8:41–56

This is the one case of raising from the dead which is included in all of the synoptic gospels. All three accounts include the story of the interruption caused by the woman who touched Jesus' clothes and was healed. Luke the doctor significantly leaves out the comment of Mark's that the woman 'had suffered much under many physicians and had spent all that she had, and was no better but rather grew worse' (5:26).

Obviously those whom Jesus raised from the dead were not given immunity from death, any more than the sick he healed were from sickness. All those whom he raised ultimately died and were buried and their bodies saw corruption. In this their experience differed from that of Jesus whose body did not see corruption. The raising of the dead was a sign of the kingdom of God. Jesus told John the Baptist that this was one of the signs that he was 'he who is to come' (Mt 11:2–6).

Notice also that all three whom Jesus raised were young people. Their deaths took place in the prime of life. It is Luke who adds the detail about Jairus' daughter, that she was

twelve years old and his only daughter, just as he tells us that
the man Jesus raised at Nain was an only son. Raising people
from the dead will always be a rarity, and the circumstances in
these two cases were exceptional. But there is something even
more important to notice. If these were all young people then
it is likely they would have lived for many years after the
gospels had been published. Since enough details are given to
identify them, they and the witnesses could easily be traced
and would, therefore, have been able to confirm or refute
these accounts. It is extremely unlikely that the writers of the
gospels would have risked telling such stories unless they had
strong evidence for them.

The critics say it is unlikely that this young girl had really
died, she had only swooned. It is true that funerals in the east
were usually held the day death took place, and it is possible
that the family and mourners were mistaken. We do not know
what the criteria for establishing when a person was 'dead'
were, and since medical science was in an early stage of
development, mistakes were no doubt made. Nevertheless it
is clear that the authors of the gospels did believe that death
had taken place. Luke tells us that the mourners knew better
when Jesus said 'she is not dead but sleeping' (Lk 8:52). They
knew she was dead. Luke also specifically tells us 'her spirit
returned' (v. 55). It would seem that Jesus used the terminology of 'sleep' to encourage the father of the girl, though he
himself knew full well what he was going to do.

All three gospels tell us about the interruption to Jesus'
walk to the house. Mark and Luke tell us that the young girl
died during that time. This interesting twist to the story
should reassure us that there are no unredeemable 'acci-
dents', nor can they ultimately hinder the will of God being
done. Jesus' work was never programmed out. He was always
flexible enough for the unexpected. The prevailing climate of
this story is strongly flavoured with unbelief. There were
those who were prepared to say 'it's too late' and 'don't
trouble Jesus any longer'. Moreover the professional mourners, who were hired for such occasions, were no doubt
hovering in the background expecting the death to take place

imminently. But in strode the Son of God, for whom it is never too late and for whom nothing is ever too much trouble. The mourners lost most of their fees, as the funeral directors did at Nain. In the presence of Jesus we should literally 'never say die', and the one who is Lord of death has absolute power to abolish it as and when he likes.

Most scholars regard this story with considerable scepticism. Plummer says we can't be sure whether the girl was dead or in a trance.[1] Leslie Weatherhead cannot accept it as a miracle.[2] Vincent Taylor[3] and Hunter[4] think she had simply been in a coma. Of course there is no way we can prove it, any more than we can prove any of the miracles of healing. In the final analysis we have to take it on faith or reject it for whatever reason we may set forward. But we are not in a position to do the same with Jesus' resurrection to which there were many witnesses and upon which the church has built its faith for nearly two thousand years.

2. The young son of the widow of Nain
   Lk 7:11–17

This is the only record we have of Jesus attending a funeral, and he stopped it! Only Luke records this story. Again we are told clearly by Luke that the young man had died. Being an only son would have added poignancy to the occasion. His probably being the only bread-winner in the family would have made the widow's future extremely bleak. The need was very great and touched the heart of Jesus so that Luke tells us that the Lord had compassion when he saw her.

He then consoled and reassured the mother and told her not to weep. To say to someone in these circumstances 'Do not weep' (v. 13) is bad advice unless you know that the reason for the weeping is about to be removed. Jesus knew instinctively, because of the intimacy of his relationship to the Father, that he was immediately to remove the cause of this woman's grief. It was typical of Jesus' personal and sensitive approach to people in real need. Luke uses an actual medical

term to describe the man 'sitting up'. Against the view that he
had only been comatosed, Luke, who gives enough details to
suggest that he had access to an eyewitness account of the
incident, says clearly that he had died, and that the dead man
sat up. The story rings true, and it is difficult to see how it
could have been sustained as authentic when the eyewitnesses
could have disproved it immediately.

3. Jesus' friend Lazarus
   Jn 11:1–44

Here the critics stand together against a story which strains
their credulity to breaking point. Many have rejected it as
unhistorical. Others believe that Lazarus was not dead but
had swooned. De Regla asserts that he was 'only in a state of
lethargy'.[5]

We are told in 12:10–11 that the chief priests also planned
to put Lazarus to death. So he too was now on their hit-list.
Since they could not refute the story they would destroy the
evidence. But there had been too many eyewitnesses for that.
The enormous crowds which welcomed Jesus into Jerusalem
on Palm Sunday were there because the news had spread like
wild-fire throughout Jerusalem and the surrounding towns
and villages. It increased the tension between Jesus and the
growing circle of his enemies enormously, and contributed
more than any other single event to his ultimate execution.

Some have doubted the story since it is not reported in the
synoptics. The silence of the other gospels is difficult to
explain, although we have already noticed that the raising of
the widow of Nain's son, which must have been widely known
amongst the apostolic band, is reported by Luke alone. Again
the synoptics are only concerned with Jesus' *Galilean* ministry, whereas the focus of John's gospel is much more on
Jerusalem.

One suggestion is that the synoptic writers suppressed this
story in order to save Lazarus' life. But this is out of harmony
with the heroic character of the early church. Tradition tells

us that Lazarus became a powerful church leader and later became Bishop of Marseilles. It is most unlikely that such an important testimony to the power and grace of God would have been silenced for such a cowardly reason. All those named in the gospels would have been at some risk; why should Lazarus be singled out for particular protection? There is no good reason why the other gospels do not record this story, which must have been known to them. It is one of the mysteries of the New Testament.

It is even more strange, if we take the view of some modern scholars (such as the late Bishop John Robinson), that John's gospel was written earlier than most scholars have agreed. Yet the fourth gospel is so different from the others we have to ask even more fundamental questions about why the gospels were written. It is inconceivable that the writer would have invented the story, since, even if we accept the later date, there would still have been eyewitnesses alive who could have refuted it, and Lazarus himself would have been the key witness. It is also so full of graphic and lifelike detail it rings true as a reliable record of an historical event. In the final analysis it is a matter of personal belief.

The story gives us a beautiful insight into this small family which had become the closest friends of Jesus and his apostolic fellowship. We don't learn too much about Lazarus himself, but we are told a lot about Mary and Martha. The characters of the two sisters are painted for us by one who obviously knew and loved them both. The reason why Jesus stayed where he was and did not immediately rush to his friend's bedside is not easy to discern. The plain answer, one supposes, is that he had not received his marching orders from the Father. But what the story brings out graphically is the way our Lord received information.

Here is another example of a word of knowledge. Jesus seemed, like the prophets in the Old Testament, to know what was going on; he received news supernaturally. So he announces 'This illness is not unto death' (v. 4), a statement which in the end proved true. There was, therefore, no need to hurry to the bedside. Then later Jesus announces, 'Our

friend Lazarus has fallen asleep . . . he is dead' (v. 11, 14).
Later he says to Martha 'Your brother will rise again' (v. 23).
In each instance action follows information which has been
conveyed to Jesus by the Holy Spirit, not by any human
means. Revelation plays an important part in the healing
ministry of Jesus. Again and again he was in possession of
knowledge hidden from most other people. He was also
prepared to act on the basis of what he had received.

There may have been other reasons for this delay. Perhaps
it was a kind of test run of his own resurrection which was to
happen on the third day. Much was at stake. The other two
raisings from the dead had taken place on the day of their
deaths, possibly within hours of the moment of death. This
was the greatest test that Jesus and the disciples had yet faced.
It was the prelude to Jesus' own death and resurrection which
were shortly to take place in Jerusalem, only a few miles from
Bethany.

We have another glimpse of Thomas the pessimist, bound
up with his own negativism. 'Let us also go,' he says, 'that we
may die with him' (v. 16). Chrysostom comments, 'he who
would hardly venture to go with him to Bethany would
afterwards without him go to India and China'.[6] This story
presents us with an extraordinary kaleidoscope of attitudes of
heart and mind. Faith rises and falls like the tides of the sea.
All that we see in the gospels about the healing ministry of
Jesus is brought into sharper than ever focus. And this is
particularly true of the two sisters. Gripped by fear and
resentment of Jesus because he had let them down by not
coming immediately to their assistance, they now believed it
was too late. It does not need much imagination to understand their feelings and trace their thoughts. Since both
Martha and Mary said the same words to Jesus ('if you had
been here, my brother would not have died', vv. 21, 32), they
had no doubt talked endlessly about the situation and re-
hearsed what they were going to say to him. For them it had
all been an 'accident'. If only Jesus had been there at the time,
Lazarus would have been healed. *They were being tested by
the discipline of divine love*. There is not necessarily any tone

of reproach in what the two sisters say to him. Mary comes quickly as soon as she knows that Jesus has arrived.

Yet the main lesson which Jesus is teaching the sisters is one that he had constantly encouraged others to see, and through it to believe and receive their healing. Martha displays a classic (but essentially unbelieving) response to a human situation into which God in Jesus Christ seeks to come. First she throws it all back into the past and blames that for the present situation. How different it would have been if Jesus had been there! In other words, healing could have happened some time in the past, but there is no confidence it will happen today. It does not matter whether the time period is a few hours, a few days or a couple of millenia. It still seems to the unbelieving heart that the Jesus who is there in the past cannot reach us today at our moment of need. Thus thousands of Christians have the most wholesome faith in what Jesus did two thousand years ago but find themselves crippled with unbelief when faced with what he might do today.

Jesus then speaks a word of faith – 'Your brother will rise again' (v. 23), meaning that day. But Martha again responds by putting the matter out of reach, though this time into the indeterminate future. 'I know he will rise again in the resurrection at the last day' (v. 24). In other words, 'it will all turn out all right in the end'. Here we see the classic 'pie in the sky when we die' approach. All our present problems are conveniently dismissed far enough away into the future to be irrelevant to our present situation. All this is looking to God who was and is to come, but who is impotent to do anything *now* on our behalf. Those who relate like this to God, are in fact banishing him to perpetual inactivity. They forget that the past was once the present, and all of the future will one day be the present. We must not leave the present to future historians. Through our faith we too are to make history.

This buck passing operation is short-circuited by Jesus in one pregnant sentence – 'I am the resurrection and the life' (v. 25). Neither Martha nor Mary could pussy-foot any longer. The friend they loved was with them, standing physically there, speaking a living faith-building word to them.

Something was going to happen in the here and now, because Jesus was there. And it is no different for us. We too live in the constant presence of the risen and glorified Lord Jesus Christ. Our faith is fortified, as the writer to the Hebrews expresses it in Hebrews 11, by the example of many generations of men and women who have done great things through the exercise of faith, often in difficult and dangerous circumstances. Neither does hope disappoint us as we look forward to the fulfilment of all the promises of God relative to the final coming of the kingdom. But that does not leave us out of consideration. We live in the present where Christ is too. He is the same today as he was yesterday, and will be forever. Faith believes in the present reality of Jesus Christ amongst his people, and both Mary and Martha ended that day knowing it to be true.

Throughout Jesus' healing ministry there runs the rich thread of compassion and concern, as well as remarkable sensitivity to people and circumstances. Some, like Schleiermacher and MacKinnon,[7] have seen this as the main reason why Jesus spent so much time with people who had diseases and sicknesses, and healed so many of them. However, it would seem there was a whole network of reasons which would have included love or compassion. Above everything Jesus was being obedient to the Father. He was doing the works the Father had given him to do. This is not in contradiction of divine love. To love people is part of that obedience, since love is commanded in both the Old and the New Testaments. We see this clearly in the story we are looking at. Throughout it Jesus is seeking to obey the Father. He moves to Bethany only when the Father tells him to. He raises the dead rather than gets there in time to heal the sick, because he is obedient. Yet the whole story is interlaced with touches of detail which brilliantly convey how deeply Jesus' emotions were involved in what he was doing. There is tenderness and anger, both legitimate emotions expressed through the humanity of the Son of God.

We are told in verse 35 that 'Jesus wept', and a different word is used to the one in verse 33 where the weeping of Mary is described. Is John telling us that Jesus' weeping is in some way different from that of Mary's? We cannot be sure what lies behind the Lord's expressions of both anger and grief. Since he knew what he was about to do, we should presume that he wept because he saw his friend Mary in tears herself. Or was he weeping because of the sinfulness and the sheer unbelief around him? He was surely weeping for Mary rather than Lazarus, whom he was about to raise from the dead anyway.

But what was the significance of Jesus being 'deeply moved in spirit and troubled' (v. 33), and being 'deeply moved again' (v. 38)? It is a very strong phrase. Jesus was experiencing something deeply within himself. Why was he so troubled? Some have suggested that it was the indignation which the Lord felt for sin. Thus Paul describes death as 'the wages of sin' (Rom 6:23). Jesus was seeing in his relationship to one of his closest earthly friends what wages had been paid out by sin.

There was a whole web of influences at work in this common human situation. There was the unbelief of the Jews and even of the sisters themselves; there was the mounting opposition to the kingdom which Jesus had come to inaugurate, so that not only were many refusing to enter it themselves, but they were actively preventing others from doing so. Bultmann believes it was the unbelief around him which caused this deep reaction in Jesus.[8] We have no need to know the answer. We are treading on delicate ground. We are peering into the very heart of Jesus. The sacredness of this should cause us to hesitate and perhaps humbly draw a veil over these words, but note in passing that the Son of God, to use the words of Hebrews, is not one 'who is unable to sympathise with our weaknesses, but one who in every respect has been tempted as we are, yet without sin' (4:15).

At the tombside Martha is still sceptical and needs further reassurances from Jesus. Her practical nature is taken up with the effects of four days of putrefaction. Jesus is concerned with something very different – 'the glory of God' (v. 40). So the miracle happens – Lazarus is called out of the grave. The

critics smile that anyone can really be so credulous as to
believe such a story. In the end it is primarily a question of
faith not scholarship.

Are the dead raised today?

Many would want to say a categorical 'no'. Many theologians
reject the historicity of the stories we have just been looking
at, or interpret them as instances of people swooning rather
than dying. Similar theories have been advanced for the
empty tomb of Jesus – namely that he had fainted on the
cross, and in the cool air of the tomb had revived and walked
out. In 1975 I was introduced to a young Christian man in
India whose name was Lazarus. I asked him why he had been
called by this name, for I had never met anyone with it before.
He told me how as a young child he had died and a coffin had
been made for him. Then through the prayers of the church he
had been raised from the dead and had also been healed. I
possess no proof that this was true. They may have been
mistaken. From time to time one hears of people reviving in
mortuaries after a doctor had certified them 'dead'. But there
are too many instances for that theory to stick.

Captain Edmund Wilbourne, a Church Army Captain, has
his own death certificate as proof of a remarkable experience
he had as a young man.[9] While still a student he developed
pneumonia and pleurisy, and was rushed into Crumpsall
Hospital in Manchester, where he was placed on the danger
list. His condition became critical and his relatives were
invited to his bedside. He lapsed into a coma and died. A
doctor signed his death certificate. His corpse was then
removed to the mortuary. Suddenly to the amazement of an
attendant working in the mortuary, he sat up and appeared to
be very much alive. He remembers to this day standing
outside his body, with a cord still linking his soul to that body.
He then had the experience of entering heaven, seeing Jesus
and a number of friends he knew who had also died. Then he
heard 'resounding through heaven a voice, at first a whisper,

which grew louder and louder. The voice was praying over and over again, "O God, don't let him die! O God, don't let him die! He has work to do for you".' Edmund recognised the voice as that of his landlady Daisy Green. He learned later that she had been kneeling by his bedside praying that very prayer. Edmund goes on, 'Jesus just smiled, turned me round by my shoulders, and gave me a push. I felt as if I was falling through space and I came to on a slab in the mortuary at the hospital . . . the attendant nearly had a heart attack!' Again one has no absolute proof. Even with modern clinical expertise it is possible to make mistakes and no one can be absolutely certain what constitutes the moment of death. But Edmund's experience is by no means unique.

Perhaps we need to approach it from another angle. If the answer to the question 'Do you believe that God raises the dead?' is 'no', then that settles the matter and we need discuss it no further. If the answer is 'yes', and particularly if we are agreed that Jesus was himself raised from the dead, can we really limit God to one generation? Why should he not do it today?

This certainly was the faith of Paul, who writes in 2 Corinthians 1:9 that we should rely 'not on ourselves but on God who raises the dead'. He is not here referring solely to Jesus' experience. He knew that this was something which God was doing and he may even have experienced it himself at Lystra (Acts 14:19). There is a clear instance of raising the dead in the ministry of Peter in Acts 9:36–43. There the people were so impressed that many believed in the Lord as a result.

It would be difficult, if we believe that the kingdom of Jesus Christ extends over all of life, to exclude from its universal sovereignty that which is most precious – the gift of life. If the Lord has the authority to take away what he has given, presumably he also has the authority to restore again what he has sovereignly taken away. Human life is something which is always in the hands of God. It is for him to do as he wishes with it.

Chapter
6

Health Restored, I

Healing, is an overall sense, is wholeness of the total person in his environment.

John Wimber

The world did not have to wait for Jesus Christ for the news that God heals. He had revealed himself as such in the desert soon after the Israelites left Egypt. God says, 'I will put none of the diseases upon you which I put upon the Egyptians; for I am the Lord, your healer' (Ex 15:26). Throughout human history disease has been spread from continent to continent by migrations of people. But here was an exception. The Jews plundered the Egyptians of their jewelry; but they took none of their diseases with them. God revealed himself to his people as the Lord of health as well as the healer of disease, the God who protects his people from disease and delivers them from its effects.

We have examined various aspects of the healing ministry of the Son of God. We have seen his purposes in coming as the supreme liberator from sin, satanic power and death itself. However, there were healings not directly related to any of these categories. The generosity of God overflowed through Jesus Christ to many people of all ages, even to Gentiles, who according to the records in the New Testament, were just sick, plain and simple. Their sicknesses were neither related to their sin nor to satanic influences.

There are twelve stories of Jesus' healings which we have so far not covered. I am dividing them into two groups. The first, which we shall deal with in this chapter, concern the stories about those handicapped by blindness, deafness, dumbness or paralysis. The second, which will be dealt with in the next chapter are the remainder of stories covering a whole range of diseases known or unknown and including the only healing from injury, when Jesus healed Malchus' ear.

Here are the healings we shall be looking at in this chapter:

1. Two blind men at Capernaum (Mt 9:27–31).
2. The blind man at Bethsaida (Mk 8:22–26).
3. Bartimaeus and his companion at Jericho (Mt 20:29–34; Mk 10: 46–52; Lk 18:35–43).
4. The deaf man with a speech defect (Mk 7:31–37).
5. The man with a withered hand (Mt 12:9–14; Mk 3:1–6; Lk 6:6–11).
6. The man at the pool of Bethesda (Jn 5:1–18).

Sickness always handicaps. Sometimes it is only a temporary setback. Sometimes it causes permanent distress and suffering. In this first group we are looking at the healings where there was chronic sickness and, as a result, permanent disability. Society is much more compassionate today towards the physically and mentally handicapped. But in those days the effects of such disabilities could be devastating. Something of the immense anxiety these people carried, and their struggle for mere existence, comes out in these stories, particularly their desperation when the possibility of healing was before them.

1. The blind men at Capernaum
Mt 9:27–31

Some indication of the harshness of public feeling towards the blind is found in the Talmud, where they are branded as dead and to be treated with disdain like lepers and the childless. This is in marked contrast to the compassionate teaching in the Old Testament (see Lev 19:14; Deut 27:18). One can begin to understand how persistently these two men solicited Jesus, their only hope of deliverance from a life of social and economic hell. There are many prophecies in Isaiah about the blind being made to see (e.g. 29:18; 35:5; 42:7, 16, 18), so we

should not be surprised that Jesus healed them in large
numbers. Blindness is a more common disability in the east
than in the west. Jesus was by no means the only person who
healed the blind. Healing claims were made by the Greeks of
Jesus' day. In Acts there are two instances of people who had
temporary blindness as a direct result of divine interventions –
Paul in Acts 9:8–19 and Elymas in Acts 13:11.

Nowhere in the gospels do we read of Jesus opening the
eyes of the blind by words of prayer. It would seem that Jesus
helps them by signs, or in this instance, by touch, for the
simple reason that they did not have the advantage others had
of seeing the Son of God. On the other hand we see here, just
as we saw in the case of the Canaanite woman (see page 47),
that Jesus tests these men's faith to the full. They follow him
crying for help. Jesus seems to ignore them altogether until he
enters a house. They are not prepared to take 'no' for an
answer, and follow him in. It is only then that he challenges
them as to whether they believe he can heal them. A simple
affirmative is all that Jesus requires. The next moment he is
touching their eyes and they are healed. So their prayers were
not immediately answered. Jesus was not always prepared
instantly to meet human need. These men had to wait, persist
in following Jesus, and go on asking until their request was
met.

Here again we find Jesus wanting to keep the healing
secret. They were told to let no one know what had happened.
The Protestant interpretation has always been that the men
were guilty of flagrant disobedience. The Catholic view has
been rather more subtle. Both Aquinas and Gregory applaud
rather than condemn these men, in spite of the fact that the
language of Jesus' embargo is very strong. The words 'sternly
charged' (*embrimaomai*, v. 30) *embrimasthai* have a note of
threatening about them. Both Aquinas and Gregory say that
Jesus never intended his words to be taken literally and they
were given out of humility, so that in fact Jesus was pleased
that they did not obey his command. This seems rather
forced. Nevertheless we should not be too hard on these men.
Their disability would have been well known and they were

no doubt beggars. It would have been hard for them to have
gone back to their friends and kept quiet about it in the face of
a barrage of questions. It would have called for a rare degree
of self-discipline and, almost certainly, removal to a place far
from their friends and families. However, we can never justify
disobedience to the commands of the Son of God.

2. The blind man at Bethsaida
   Mk 8:22–26

Bethsaida, together with its near neighbour Capernaum, was
strongly criticised by Jesus Christ. In Matthew 11:20–24 he
condemned these cities for their unbelief and their lack of
repentance. He said it would be more tolerable on the day of
judgement for the land of Sodom than for them (v. 24).
Bethsaida, like Capernaum was a prosperous city, a fishing
port on the shores of the Lake of Galilee. Affluence seldom
provides good soil in which to grow faith, and these cities saw
no need for repentance or faith in the gospel.

   Mark is the only one of the gospel writers to record this
story. There are three interesting aspects to it, one of which is
unique amongst the healings of Jesus. This blind person,
unlike Bartimaeus, did not come to Jesus of his own accord.
He was brought by others who begged Jesus to heal him.
Calvin, commenting on this story, says that Jesus was 'not
bound by fixed rules but can show his power both in this way
and in that.'[1] It illustrates yet again that Jesus was never
bound by any techniques in his healing ministry. The variety
of approaches he made seems endless. He treated each
person differently, thus recognising the individuality of each
person and respecting it. It also demonstrates Jesus' total
dependence on the Holy Spirit. Each healing was an original
masterpiece.

   Secondly, this healing was gradual. Others of the healings
of Jesus may also have been. But this is the only one we are
specifically told was of this nature. It is interesting in the light
of the fact that most modern examples of divine healing are

gradual rather than immediate, although it is not always possible to be sure whether a healing is gradual or not. The symptoms, for example, may take longer to clear up than the disease itself. How can one be sure, for example, in cases like cancer and various forms of heart disease, when there may be a long gap between tests? But here is a case of gradual healing.

There is something distinctly warm and human about this story. The healing is not the work of some remote guru who from his throne of power waves his magic wand over the sufferings of mankind. Jesus ministers carefully and sympathetically to this man. He gives him a helpful sign by spitting on his eyes and laying his hands on him.

It is worth pausing for a moment and looking more closely at the significance of Jesus' use of spittle. There are two other examples of Jesus using it in the process of healing in John 9:6 and Mark 7:33. The history of the symbolism of spitting is fascinating. From the beginning it conveyed deep enmity (Num 12:14), and Christ himself has to submit to this indignity as 'the suffering servant' (Isa 50:6; Mt 26:67). The Essenes punished it by a thirty-day penance. But in Jesus' day both Jews and Greeks used it as a healing technique.[2]

With the coming of Christ what had been a sign of enmity became one of grace, and the practice of spittle can be found in baptismal rites in Rome and Milan. Today there is no question that to spit on a person is one of the most insulting of actions. How interesting that Jesus turned a curse into a blessing through his use of spittle. Is this not typical of Jesus' ministry, which reached its climax when the curse of being hanged on a tree became the most powerful sign in the world for forgiveness and cleansing? One can begin to understand through this the scandal of the gospel; what was cursed became in Jesus the very source of endless blessings.

There is an interesting description by Vincent Donovan in his book *Christianity Rediscovered* of the use of spittle amongst the Masai tribes of Tanzania.[3] When a son was estranged from his father he would be encouraged to ask for the 'spittle of forgiveness'. Spittle for the Masai is regarded as a very sacred element of a living, breathing human and the sign of forgiveness. It is an African sacrament, for it is more than a mere sign. It is for them forgiveness, and is a sign of blessing not cursing.

Another interesting feature of this unique story is the way Jesus took the blind man by the hand and led him out of the village (8:23). It is not too hard to see the reason for this. We have already seen how unbelieving this village was. It was singled out by Jesus for outspoken criticism. The atmosphere in the place was not the least bit conducive to a faithful response on the part of the blind man. So Jesus took him away from this unbelieving environment. We have already seen the mistake the disciples made when they tried to combine dialogue with the lawyers and a healing work (see page 42). Theological discussion and being surrounded by sceptics makes healing impossible. We need to remember that when Jesus went to his own home town of Nazareth we are told 'he could do no mighty work there' (Mk 6:5), and Matthew adds, 'because of their unbelief' (Mt 13:58). Even Jesus was prevented from healing the sick when surrounded by either hostile, apathetic or sceptical crowds.

3. Bartimaeus and his companion at Jericho
   Mt 20:29–34; Mk 10:46–52; Lk 18:35–43

All the gospels agree that Jesus was on his final journey to Jerusalem and that a large crowd was following him. His ministry of miracles was nearly over, and for some time he had been trying to avoid crowds. Now his eyes were fixed on Jerusalem and the final test. Suddenly there came wafting to him amidst the normal confused noises of the crowd the cries of the needy. Jesus had the gift of being immediately able to pick out the personal cry for help from the hubbub of the multitudes. Just as the touch of a woman who needed healing was immediately recognised by him, even when hundreds of others were pressing upon him (see page 100), so he heard the cries of the blind beggars while his ears were deaf to the babble of the crowds that pressed around him. Some years ago on Madras station we were thronged by dozens of young Indian boys begging for money. The missionary seeing us off scanned the shining faces of these boys and saw one who was near to starvation. As our train pulled out of the station we saw him single this young lad from all the others and take him off to give him some food. Likewise Jesus was able instinctively to distinguish real human need from mere human interest.

The men's cries provoked opposition. As with the Canaanite woman (see page 47) people around them tried to silence them, which only encouraged them to shout even louder (how human!). Faith often has to overcome barriers like this. We sometimes have to come struggling to Jesus. For various reasons people may not want us to come, and we have to wrestle with the well-meaning opposition. It may have been their cry 'Son of David' which upset the people. Whatever it was, the beggars were rebuked.

All three gospels agree on Jesus' reaction to this. They tell us 'he stopped'. It is one of the most moving statements in the gospels. The normal impression of great people is one of hyper-activism; they fulfil a whirlwind of engagements, rushing from one crowd of people to the next. Their leisure moments, if they have any, are spent on themselves. But here Jesus stopped on his way to the most important appointment any person has ever had to keep. He did it for poor blind beggars. He singled them out from the crowd and gave them his valuable time.

The gospels also agree that Jesus asked them 'What do you want me to do for you?', which must have appeared at the time a rather strange question. But it was again typical of our Lord that he always wanted people to be specific not general in their requests, just as he was always specific in his own prayer for the sick and suffering. There may be a place for general prayers. Yet in these situations Jesus required something specific. He got it – 'Lord, let our eyes be opened' (Matt 20:33), and they got their healing. Then Jesus resumed his uphill journey to Jerusalem and to death and glory.

4. The deaf man with a speech defect
   Mk 7:31–37

There are a number of interesting pointers in this story to the effectiveness of Jesus' healing work. One is that Jesus did not do what he was asked to do. In verse 32 he was asked to lay his hands on him. He didn't comply. It is a warning to all engaged in a healing ministry. People often come to us, as they come to doctors, telling us what they think is the problem. Then they tell us what we should do about it. A good doctor will listen but not necessarily agree with what is being said. In the healing ministry it is crucial to try to hear what the Holy Spirit is saying about the disease or sickness a person may have, and the method the same Holy Spirit wants us to follow in praying for and ministering to them. We should never feel bound to agree with any suggested diagnosis nor to do what we are asked to do by the patient or their friends.

Many times people have come to me to ask for healing, expecting prayer and the laying-on of hands. Instead I have been guided by the Holy Spirit to give them medical, moral or psychological advice, which has led to their healing. The onset of heart disease, for example, may be held back through sensible dieting, if a person is overweight, and arthritis can be healed when resentments and bitternesses are confessed and renounced. Jesus' success was due to his obeying the Father, not just doing what people asked him to do.

It would seem from v. 35 that this person's speech defect (he could not speak 'plainly') was affected by his deafness. He was probably unable to speak well rather than actually being dumb. The Greek word can mean either 'dumb' or having a speech defect (even being a stammerer). Again we see Jesus ministering privately (v. 33) rather than publicly to this man. Jesus was always sensitive about the right way to minister. He did it the way that was best for each individual. It seems clear that this man could not have responded as he did if it had been done in the full glare of an excited crowd. So Jesus took him off on his own. Jesus dealt with the deafness first, because that was the probable cause of the speech defect. This incident took place in the same region as the Gadarene demoniac (see Mk 5:1–20 and page 40) – but there is no mention of demonic activity in this case. Here Jesus ordered the crowd to 'tell no one' about what had happened, in contrast to the demoniac who was told to share the good news of his healing with his friends and relatives. Jesus not only varied his methods, but also the instructions he issued to those he healed and those who witnessed such miracles.

The preservation of the actual Aramaic word *ephphatha* 'be opened', in verse 34 (as also *talitha cumi* in Mk 5:41) is interesting. It suggests the narrative of an eyewitness who actually remembered the words of power which were used. The language of 'opening' was later transferred to the rite of baptism in the early church to signify the removal by the Spirit of the inward obstacles of the mind (see also Acts 16:14 where the opening of the heart is mentioned).

5. The man with a withered hand
   Mt 12:9–14; Mk 3:1–6; Lk 6:6–11

Jesus is again on a collision course with the Pharisees. He heals a man who has a withered hand in a synagogue on the sabbath. He offends the religious establishment so much that they begin to plan ways of destroying him (Mk 3:6). It is one of no less than seven recorded cures performed by Jesus on the sabbath (Mk 1:21; Mk 1:29; Mk 3:2; Lk 13:14; Lk 14:1; Jn 5:9; Jn 9:14).

The gospel writers are concerned to show that Jesus' healing ministry was in the centre of the life of the community of God's people. Where better to heal the sick than in the synagogue and what better day than the sabbath, the commemoration of the completion of the work of creation? Sickness disturbs the work of the creator. Healing restores it. This all makes good sense, but not to the Pharisees, who interpreted it as 'work' and, therefore, an infringement of the laws of the sabbath.

The gospels make it clear that the Pharisees were setting

Jesus up for this; they may even have planted the man there for this purpose. They hoped Jesus would do what he did and thereby infringe the law and give them the chance of accusing him. Mark and Luke specifically tell us that they were watching Jesus 'to see whether he would heal him on the sabbath, so that they might accuse him' (Mk 3:2; Lk 6:7). Luke adds the fact that Jesus 'knew their thoughts'. Jesus was not taken in by the trap that had been set for him. He knew intuitively what they were planning. And he had an answer to their stratagem which made *them* rather than him a laughing stock in the synagogue that day.

In the first place Jesus knew the law better than they did. Even the Talmud said, 'the sabbath is in your hands, not you in the hands of the sabbath'. God's law was never intended to be interpreted the way the Pharisees did. Jesus' task was to convert bondage to liberty and to turn people's attention from the shadow to the substance and from the letter to the spirit. Augustine writes, 'he, the light, had come; he was now removing the shadows'. But, secondly, we find Jesus acting with consummate cleverness. Normally he would have laid his hands on the sick (which could have been interpreted as 'work'). Here he simply spoke a healing word and got the man to do all the work! Jesus didn't even walk towards the man, he told him to come and stand by him. While his enemies watched for him to do the offending action they were amazed instead to hear him issue a simple and direct command 'Stretch out your hand' (Lk 6:10). No wonder we are told they were 'filled with fury' (Lk 6:11)! Their carefully prepared plans were frustrated. Jesus had out-manoeuvred them and they were mad at him.

The healing teaches us something else too. Jesus' healing ministry was free from techniques and gimmicks. The one who came to release mankind from the narrow legalism with which his enemies had enslaved the community of God's people, had no intention of substituting for it another form of legalism, binding his followers to rules and regulations related to healing sick people. So Jesus was prepared to adjust his methods to the prevailing situation. The important thing was to heal the sick and, on the way to achieve this goal, to make it as simple as possible for people to believe. The weaker a person's faith, the easier Jesus made it for them to believe.

Here we find Jesus doing nothing except giving a short command. The man had to stretch out his withered hand. He had to do something which was impossible. He had to put flesh to his faith. Believing and acting on the basis of faith, are often linked in the stories of the miracles in the New Testament. Peter had to walk on the water, the disciples had to distribute the loaves and fishes, the men had to let the paralysed person down through the roof and this man had to stretch out his hand before he was healed. In the act of doing it, he was healed. Faith, in this case, was not waiting for something to happen; it was doing something believing it would happen. There is the world of difference between these two attitudes, and there is no question which one the Lord commended, and through which he worked his healing gifts.

6. The man at the pool of Bethesda
   Jn 5:1–18

History abounds with stories of the discovery of healing waters or springs. Since the last century Lourdes in Southern France has become the most famous. On 11 February 1858 Bernadette Soubirous, then aged fourteen, had a vision of the Virgin Mary near the Massabieille grotto. It is not surprising that the element of water, with its symbolism of purification and life is so often associated with healing properties.

Throughout the healing ministry of Jesus we have that strong sense that he had spiritual insights which enabled him to see things to which most people were blind. This was one of the most important features of all that he did, and accounted largely for the successful outcome of his ministry on each occasion. This story is a classic example of the sovereignty principle which is to be seen in every incident. On some occasions he healed everyone. On this, he only healed one person out of many. Why this man? Jesus answers this question himself in a discourse later in this chapter, 'I can do nothing on my own authority; as I hear, I judge; and my judgement is just, because I seek not my own will but the will of him who sent me' (v. 30). Jesus listened and heard this man's name and no one else's called by the Father.

But there is another important aspect of Jesus' healing ministry which is highlighted here, the manifestation of the gift of the word of knowledge, or the supernatural awareness of facts which are normally hidden from us. We are told that Jesus 'knew that he had been lying there a long time' (v. 6). Some modern commentators suggest that he obtained this information by asking some of the other sick people. This is a possibility, but the more likely explanation is that it was a word of knowledge. As Jesus' eyes fell on this particular man he knew immediately that he was a chronic sufferer and, indeed, a great deal more about him as we shall see. Modern commentators have a tendency to look for rational explanations whenever possible and to discount any spiritual explanations of what happened.

This story includes several elements which keep recurring in Jesus' healing ministry. One of them is in the question addressed to this man, 'Do you want to be healed?' (v. 6). Jesus wanted to move people to a place of faith, built on a strong motivation and determination to be healed. This is particularly important in the case of the chronically sick, who after time become so adjusted to their physical limitations they often do not want to have their circumstances changed. To want to be healed is an essential prerequisite for it to happen. This man saw Jesus as a helper rather than a healer. Perhaps he could help him into the water when the mad scramble took place as the waters 'moved'. The man was evidently surprised at the sudden command 'Rise, take up your pallet, and walk' (v. 8). The shock may have contributed to the cure. A theological or pastoral lecture would have been out of place. The sudden and unexpected command broke through years of acceptance of a chronic condition. He was instantly healed and took up his pallet and walked.

But there are two other factors in this story which crop up in

others. We have already mentioned the question of sin. Sin
was a factor in this man's condition, or Jesus would not have
said later, 'Sin no more, that nothing worse befall you'
(v. 14). Loos points out that Jesus was not interested in
physical healing alone, and so took the matter further.[4] We
need to see that the link between sickness and sin is sometimes there.

A much stronger factor in this story is the alleged sabbath-
breaking background to it. Jesus moves majestically through
the tangled undergrowth of Jewish legalism to establish the
divine principle that man's well-being is more important than
a scrupulous observance of the law, and in any case the law
was introduced for man's benefit not vice versa. It was an
absurd accusation. Taking up the pallet was interpreted as
'work'. But the incident was the tip of an iceberg. For Jesus
was challenging the authority of the Pharisees and showing up
their pride and hypocrisy.

John's gospel, as we have seen before, abounds in symbolism. Stories are recorded to illustrate great principles, and it is
done systematically. Cullmann sees John as seeking 'to set
forth the connexion between the contemporary Christian
worship and the historical life of Jesus'.[5] He therefore points
to sacramental traces which Bultmann, on the other hand,
believes John had no interest in. C. H. Dodd stresses the
symbolic element in the fourth gospel and the conflict between law and the words and works of Jesus.[6] At Bethesda
the water fails to bring healing. Nothing happens to this man
for thirty-eight years. The Torah promised life, but only Jesus
saves. Dodd writes, 'The law might show the way of life: it was
powerless to create the will to live. The will to live, together
with the power to live, is given in the word of Christ.'[7]

Some of the church fathers saw this healing as a symbol of
baptism. The addition to the text in verses 3–4 was seen as
part of this symbolism. Tertullian spoke of a 'baptismal
angel',[8] and Chrysostom took a similar line. In one of his
Easter messages he speaks eloquently of the power of the
gospel in contrast to the miserably inefficient waters at
Bethesda: 'Didst thou cast the whole world into these

spiritual fountains the grace would not be worn out, the gift expended, the fountains defiled, the liberality exhausted.'[9]

When we have reflected on all this, and no doubt much more, and have looked at all possible interpretations of the rich symbolical details, the story reveals the work of a master who not only knew what was in man, but also had the grace and power to heal a chronically sick person, and command him immediately to supply to the whole world concrete evidence that he was completely well again.

Chapter
7

In this chapter we shall examine the healing stories which don't seem to fit into any particular category:

1. The man with dropsy (Lk 14:1–6).
2. The woman with frequent haemorrhaging (Mt 9:20–22; Mk 5:25–34; Lk 8:43–48).
3. The centurion's servant (Mt 8:5–13; Lk 7:1–10).
4. The nobleman's son (Jn 4:46–54).
5. Peter's mother-in-law (Mt 8:14–15; Mk 1:29–31; Lk 4:38–39).
6. Malchus' ear (Mt 26:51–52; Mk 14:47; Lk 22:49–51; Jn 18:10–11).

1. The man with dropsy
Lk 14:1–6

There is a distinct similarity between this story and the one described in chapter three (page 48), the woman with the bent back (Lk 13:10–17). It is true the setting is different. The woman's healing takes place in the synagogue, the man's in the house of one of the leaders of the Pharisees. The causes were also different; the woman was 'bound by Satan', whereas there is no cause mentioned for the man's disease. But the similarities are striking. Both these healings took place on the sabbath. Both were opposed for that reason. In both cases the opposition was defeated. In the case of the woman in the synagogue we are told, 'all his adversaries were put to shame',

(13:17) and in the other case 'they were silent' (14:4). There are hints that in both incidents the sick people were 'planted' by Jesus' enemies to lure him into a trap.

Perhaps the most striking similarity is Jesus' use of apt illustrations to confound his enemies. Since the woman was 'bound by Satan', Jesus speaks of the common practice of loosing animals and leading them away to be watered (13:15). Surely people are more important than animals, is Jesus' argument. But with the man suffering from dropsy Jesus changes the illustration to an ox or an ass falling into a well of water. The main feature of dropsy is the increase in water content in the body, so that the patient virtually 'drowns' in it. Both pictures are very telling.

There is a hint in this story that the man was deliberately 'planted' by being invited to dinner that night, in the hope that Jesus would heal him. If he did so he would demonstrate his disregard for the sabbath laws, an accusation which was constantly being made against him. The text tells us that 'they were watching him' (v. 1). The Living Bible interprets it to mean that they had an ulterior motive in inviting this man to dinner; 'the Pharisees were watching him like hawks to see if he would heal a man there who was suffering from dropsy' is how it is translated. If that is true then Jesus walked straight into their cunningly conceived trap, but, as always, turned it to his own advantage. Jesus was always on a collision course when it came to conflicts between the law and its interpretation. The real battle was between two different interpretations of the uses of the law. The Pharisees and legal experts believed in law for its own sake. Jesus went deeper and further and saw law as man's servant not his master. Jesus never spoke against the law, though later he was to be accused of just that. But when it came to interpreting it, he took the view that the law was there for man's blessing, not to be obeyed for its own sake.

The Talmud compared dropsy with leprosy. It was a matter of the equal balance between water and blood in the human body. If there was more water, then dropsy was the result; if more blood, then leprosy. The cause of dropsy was sometimes linked to sexual offences. Dropsy affected the knee joints and this would explain why we are told that Jesus 'took him' (v. 4). Literally Jesus helped him to his feet and then healed him.

This was not the first occasion when Jesus' enemies were silenced (v. 4). They were not prepared to risk public exposure and ridicule by answering Jesus' searching question. When he asked them a second question we are told 'they could not reply to this' (v. 6). Archbishop Trench comments, 'they were silenced, but not convinced; and the truth which did not win them, did the only other thing which it could do, exasperated them the more'.[1] That is what truth always does to us. It convinces us or exasperates us if we reject it.

2. The woman with frequent haemorrhaging
   Mt 9:20–22; Mk 5:25–34; Lk 8:43–48

Here is a story which illustrates the overflowing of the grace of God seen in the ministry of our Lord Jesus Christ. As he moves quickly to accomplish one work of grace, he performs another on the journey. The disciples realise that Jesus is on an emergency call. A young girl is desperately ill. They express their irritation when Jesus stops suddenly and attends to this woman's needs. Jesus was ready for surprises. His programme was always open-ended. He was prepared to be interrupted if need be. His sensitivity to the Holy Spirit is never more perfectly illustrated than in this incident, for obviously speed was of the essence if Jairus' daughter was to be healed. Actually she died before they got there; but death was to prove no barrier to the will of God being done. This story highlights how ready Jesus was to feel the touch of someone in need in the midst of a crowded programme and during one of his many 'walkabouts' when thousands touched him ceaselessly. Jesus knew the difference between the touch of the inquisitive or the casually superstitious and that of a person desperate for healing.

At first glance this story appears to run counter to the

principles upon which Jesus based his healing work. The woman takes the initiative. She breaks the laws relating to hygiene. She pushes through the crowd with the one aim of touching Jesus and getting what she wants, her healing, without bothering him further. Greydanus argues that Jesus was wanting to protect the woman's peace of mind.[2] Plummer also believes that Jesus knew exactly what was going on.[3] Strauss, however, believes that Jesus didn't know and he likens the incident to 'a charged battery which discharges itself when touched'.[4] Loos believes the question was a real one and that Jesus genuinely registered surprise.[5] It is fun to speculate in this way, but we just don't know the answer.

This is one of a number of mentions in the gospels of people touching Jesus' clothing for healing. In Matthew 14:36 we are told that the sick besought Jesus, 'that they might only touch the fringe of his garment; and as many as touched it were made well' (see also Mark 6:56). In Mark 3:10 we are told 'all who had diseases pressed upon him to touch him'. In Luke 6:19, 'all the crowd sought to touch him, for power came forth from him and healed them all'. All these references, together with this story, show how many people believed that a mere touch would do the trick. Even today there is much popular belief that to touch someone or something holy will be beneficial and bring healing or some other benefit. A few years ago my wife and I were speaking at a conference in Madras, South India. On the first evening Mother Theresa of Calcutta was to speak. A crowd of over 15,000 people showed up to hear her. But so did the police and units of the Indian army. Crush barriers were erected and it was made clear that it would be impossible to approach the platform. Many would have wanted to get close to this woman who has such a reputation in India; and even, if possible, touch her. The police and army made sure that this frail old lady would be protected from what could have been dangerous mobbing. So too in Jesus' day the sick tried to lay their hands on him to touch him.

What is important for us to grasp is that it was not the touch that healed this woman. Jesus himself made this plain. All three gospels concur that Jesus said, 'Daughter, your *faith* has made you well; go in peace' (Lk 8:48). Although the woman was wrong to think that a touch of Jesus would be enough, it still worked! But it was her faith, not her touching of Jesus, which healed her. There was probably an element of superstition in the woman's mind. Her action was morally dubious. But Jesus wasn't worried about the negatives. There was enough positive faith, and particularly the ingenuity of true faith, to give her what she wanted. In the other incidents, quoted in the last paragraph, in which we are told that many sick people sought to touch Jesus Christ, it never actually says that the touch itself produced the healing. It was the faith which brought them to touch the Lord that was effective, not the physical touch itself.

For faith to operate people need a point of contact. Oral Roberts realised this many years ago. On radio and in his TV programmes he asked the sick to touch their radio or television sets. It was a point of contact. It helped them to an act of faith. None of these men believed or taught that there were magic properties in these sets. It was faith that would heal them; but faith needs a point of contact. At times there is only a short step between faith and superstition. Jesus always understood human frailty. But this story bears out that it is better to believe too much than too little.

It is clear that in Jesus' healing ministry the will of God was paramount. But there always has to be a balance between the divine will and human responsibility. In John's gospel Jesus expressed that balance in the words, 'All that the Father gives me will come to me (predestination); and him who comes to me (freewill), I will not cast out' (6:37). We have already noticed how selective Jesus was at the pool of Bethesda. Only one was healed out of many, and Jesus selected who it should be. In contrast, in this story all the initiative comes from the human side. Jesus seems to have been taken by surprise. The woman gets her healing before Jesus even knows who she is.

This story is comforting to those who feel that no one has got any time for them, least of all God. It is challenging also to

those who are too busy and whose lives are too programmed.
Jesus always seemed to find time to deal with genuine human
need, and so should we.

3. The centurion's servant
   Mt 8:5–13; Lk 7:1–10

Both Matthew and Luke record this story about the healing of
the centurion's slave. Some commentators, such as Loos,
believe that the Johannine passage (4:46–54) is another
parallel.[6] But the details of this story are so different it is hard
to believe John is telling us about the same incident. In the
synoptic version the sick person is a slave, in the Johannine a
son although the Greek word *pais* can double for both. There
is no mention of a centurion. John describes the person as an
'official'. It is true the town of Capernaum is specifically
mentioned in all three accounts. Also the healings take place
without Jesus actually being present. Nevertheless the whole
feel of the Johannine story is totally different and, therefore,
in this book will be dealt with separately.

Both Matthew and Luke see this story as one which exposes
the unbelief of the Jews and is a preview of the opening of
salvation's doors to the whole Gentile world. Matthew records the words of Jesus about those who would come from
all over the world and 'sit at table with Abraham, Isaac,
and Jacob in the kingdom of heaven, while the sons of
the kingdom will be thrown into the outer darkness . . .'
(8:11–12).

It is hard to fault this centurion. He seems almost too good
to be true. He displays a remarkable Christlikeness even
though he had probably not met Jesus before. He is a man of
great love. He obviously cared for his slave, which was
unusual for those days. Slaves were the property of their
masters. The Roman writer Cicero once apologised for feeling deeply the death of a slave. We are also told by Luke that
the elders informed Jesus that 'he loves our nation' (7:5).
Apparently he built the Jews a synagogue. The Roman army

of occupation despised the Jewish nation, regarding it as a
tin-pot country compared with the mighty Roman empire.
Unlike many Romans, particularly those occupying the land
of Israel, he was also a man of deep humility. The juxtapo-
sition of the elders' statement about him ('he is worthy') and
his own opinion about himself ('I am not worthy') is striking
(Lk 7:4, 6). He was not prepared to take advantage of the high
opinion the Jewish leaders had of him, nor of his status in the
Roman army, to seek to influence Jesus in any way.

But it is his respect for authority which is the most important aspect of this man's life, and the key to the healing
which was about to take place. He accepts Jewish protocol
and sends the elders of the Jews to Jesus. In James 5:14 we see
an interesting parallel to this, when the elders of the church
are to be called to minister to the sick. But that is not the main
point. It would seem that the centurion knew something
about Jesus' authority. We are told (Luke 7:3) that he had
'heard of Jesus'. It had been reported to him that Jesus spoke
and ministered to people with authority. A person who has
real authority is a man of few words. Long and elaborate
sentences are a sign of weakness, and unbelief. The centurion understood this from his military training. One word
is enough. 'Go' or 'come' is sufficient to move whole armies.
All Jesus, therefore, needed to do was to 'say the word'. Perhaps it had been reported to him that Jesus sometimes healed
people with only one word, for example, 'Be opened'
(*ephphatha*, Mk 7:34); or that he cast out devils with a word
(Mt 8:16). Bengel sees in this man the wisdom of faith which
comes from 'military abruptness'.[7]

For this man authority and faith belonged together. He
knew that this was the way Jesus operated. Faith was based on
the authority that had been given. It was because Jesus was a
man 'under authority' that he was able to have authority in his
ministry to the sick and the demonised. This was the measure
of the centurion's faith. Jesus had only to speak a word and his
slave would be healed. Augustine comments, 'the centurion
did not receive him into his house, but he had received him
already into his heart. The more humble, the more capacious;

"for the hills drive back the water, but the valleys are filled by it".[8]

There are only two occasions in the gospels when we are told that Jesus registered surprise. One is when he visited his home town of Nazareth and could do no powerful work there. We are told that 'he marvelled because of their unbelief' (Mk 6:6). The other is in this story. In the first example Jesus was expecting faith, but found to his surprise, unbelief. In this case Jesus was not expecting faith from a Roman soldier, but to his surprise found it. He marvelled when he saw and heard it. 'I tell you,' he said, 'not even in Israel have I found such faith' (Lk 7:9).

It is an interesting fact that all the references to centurions in the New Testament show them in a favourable light (e.g. Mt 27:54; Lk 23:47; Acts 10:22; 22:26; 23:18; 24:23; 27:43). In the growing moral decay of the Roman empire, the army was one of the few institutions where some of the old virtues survived. A centurion's position in the middle of the military hierarchy meant he had to maintain the highest discipline and moral integrity. Here was a man, for all his military qualities, who, according to Bernard, 'poured the oil of his compassion into the vessel of faith'.[9]

4. The nobleman's son
Jn 4:46–54

It has been suggested by some that this man was Chuza, Herod's steward, whose wife is named amongst the women who provided for Jesus and the disciples (Lk 8:3). This is a different incident from the preceding one, although there is one important common factor – the person healed was not present at the time. Jesus simply spoke words of authority, and the healing took place. Jesus also delivered someone from evil spirits at a distance, when he set free the daughter of the Canaanite woman (Mt 15:21–28). We have, therefore, grounds for believing that the same can happen today, and a point of contact is not essential. We need, however, to

balance this with the fact that the vast majority of Jesus'
healings took place through personal contact with the patient.
With the Canaanite woman and the Roman centurion an
extraordinary level of faith was present, so a 'point of contact'
was unnecessary.

In this story Jesus said words which would have offended
and discouraged most people, 'Unless you see signs and
wonders you will not believe' (v. 48). Jesus did not want a
faith that believed in miracles for their own sake. There
comes from this man, in answer to this statement, a heart cry
which produced an immediate response from Jesus, 'Sir,
come down before my child dies' (v. 49). Jesus does not pray
specifically for this man's son. He simply declares what has
happened, 'Go; your son will live' (v. 50). It is more like a
word of knowledge or a prophetic statement. Such gifts,
properly used through the inspiration of the Holy Spirit, do
produce this kind of result. They bring into being what is said.
This is further proof of the important place that prophetic
statements and words of knowledge have in the healing
ministry.

John is concerned to show his readers just how effective
Jesus' words were. It was discovered later that at the exact
moment Jesus had spoken these words the fever left this
young man. But John also wants us to realise the power of
signs and wonders and their influence on people's faith. He
tells us that when the official got home and realised what had
happened 'he himself believed and all his household' (v. 53).
John recalls the same effect at Cana when the water was
turned into wine. He tells us that as a direct result of that
miracle, 'his disciples believed in him' (2:11). This is the main
reason why this gospel was written, and why the signs are
recorded (20:31).

It is fascinating to see the stages through which this man
passed to reach faith. He begins with faith in Jesus' miraculous power (v. 47). He has to receive a 'course correction'
from Jesus which takes him on a stage further into sheer
compassionate concern (v. 49). When he realises that his son
has been healed through the word of Jesus, then he reaches a

stage of faith for himself and his family. Bultmann and others see the man becoming a Christian when he comes to that third stage recorded in verse 53.[10]

It is interesting to contrast this healing with that of the centurion's slave. In the case of the centurion we see a strong faith crowned and rewarded. In this story we see a narrow and poor faith enlarged and deepened. Chrysostom contrasts the way in which Jesus offers to go to the centurion's house and thus brings out and honours the centurion's humility, with this story when he refuses to go and thus increases the man's faith. For the centurion a word was enough; this man demanded Jesus' presence. Bishop Hall compares the two stories and writes of the one as 'a ceding to loftiness' and the other 'a conceding to lowliness of mind'.[11]

Capernaum was some distance from Cana, so this man would have had quite a journey ahead of him. The Greek makes it clear that he proceeded home at a leisurely pace, which is a further indication of the faith which he had. As the scripture says, 'He who believes will not be in haste' (Isa 28:16). Yet his faith was still not complete. As he met his servants he asked them 'the hour when he began to mend' (v. 52). This would indicate that he was not expecting an immediate healing, but a slow and gradual one. When he realised the full extent of the healing, and how it had been immediate and complete, he was ready, together with his household, to believe in a way which had not been evident before. So faith grows as a seed from small beginnings to its fullest extent and maturity.

5. Peter's mother-in-law
   Mt 8:14–15; Mk 1:29–31; Lk 4:38–39

This was one of the earliest healings of Jesus. According to Matthew Jesus touched her hand. Mark says he took her by the hand, whereas Luke is more dramatic – he stood over her and rebuked the fever. He could well have done all three, and each of the gospel writers wants to highlight one in particular.

Touching, lifting up by the hand and rebuking are three methods often employed by Jesus. Luke alone tells us it was 'a high fever' (4:38), which would suggest it was more than influenza or a common cold, perhaps it was even typhus.

In this incident there was no period of convalescence. The sick woman was healed and got up immediately to serve the disciples. Sometimes it has been argued that Jesus' healings were so complete that there was never any need for convalescence afterwards. This has been used as evidence that Jesus' healing ministry was unique and not to be compared with the modern healing movement in which a period of convalescence is usually required. But such comparisons are misleading. In the first place we are simply not told what happened afterwards to many of those whom Jesus healed. Some may have needed convalescence, others may have experienced a gradual healing. Some modern healings through faith in Jesus Christ have in my experience needed no convalescence and been instantaneous. Margery Stevens, an English woman, was instantly healed during the advanced stages of multiple sclerosis. This took place in the early morning, and she not only cooked her mother's breakfast for her that same day, but went round after breakfast to report her healing to her doctor. It is true that some instances of modern healing are gradual. But it is jumping to conclusions to surmise that all Jesus' healings were like this one. There is no clear evidence since the follow-up to most of them is not documented.

Matthew's account of this incident is followed by a general statement about the events which followed that same day. In the evening Jesus had to cope with many demon possessed people who were brought to him. We are told he cast them out 'with a word' (8:16) and 'healed all who were sick'. It is not clear whether sick people were also brought or whether the reference is to the demon possessed. Throughout his gospel Matthew is keen to reveal Jesus as the fulfiller of the prophecies of the Old Testament. Here he tells us that Jesus was fulfilling Isaiah 53:4, 'He took our infirmities and bore our diseases' (8:17).

Many Pentecostals claim that healing is 'in the atonement' and this verse is quoted in support. Isaiah 53 is mentioned elsewhere in the New Testament as being fulfilled in the death of Jesus Christ. Isaiah 53:5, for example, which is also linked by some to the healing ministry of Jesus, is quoted in 1 Peter 2:24, though not in the context of healing. The difficulty with the use of Isaiah 53:4 is to see how it could have been fulfilled, as the quotation states, in Jesus' delivering Peter's mother-in-law from a fever and many from evil spirits, since the atonement had not then taken place. Also Isaiah 53:4 speaks of a vicarious bearing of sicknesses. There is no mention of Jesus being sick at this point. He was certainly empathising; he was being drained as he gave of himself, or as it was put later 'virtue' was going out of him. But he wasn't actually, at that moment, taking the sicknesses upon himself.

However puzzling this may seem, we have to realise that these are the comments of someone writing after the death of Christ. We must understand too that sin and sickness are very closely related in the New Testament, and it is inconceivable to imagine Jesus dying for our sins and not dying for our sicknesses. Nevertheless we also need to realise that sin is not sickness *per se*, nor is sickness always due to personal sin. There are promises which declare that sin has been dealt with by Jesus and that through repentance and faith there is an instant cleansing without a period of divine probation; whereas sicknesses are not so easily dealt with even when there is personal repentance and faith. The two cannot be linked together as if they are the same. But the victory of Christ on the cross, which is so clearly prophesied in Isaiah 53, must include within its huge and cosmic scope our sicknesses and spiritual bondages. In that sense Matthew is right to link what Jesus had just done with what he had primarily come to do at Calvary. Jesus came to heal the sick as well as deliver us from sin and satanic power. Our mandate for believing and practising the truth of this comes from the cross of Jesus and every victory won in this realm is another fulfilment of Isaiah 53:4.

6. Malchus' ear
Mt 26:51–52; Mk 14:47; Lk 22:49–51; Jn 18:10–11.

This has been hailed as the only surgical miracle that Jesus performed. Recent developments in the field of micro-surgery have made this kind of healing fairly commonplace. There are, however, a number of problems associated with the accounts given by the gospel writers.

The main difficulty is that only Luke records the *healing*. The other gospels refer to the *incident*, recall the severing of the ear, but make no mention of a healing. This is all the more surprising since the three gospels which are silent about the healing are those whose authors would have been eye-witnesses or close to those who were, whereas Luke was certainly not present, yet records the healing.

There are a number of authentic touches which would indicate the veracity of the story, not least that all four gospels record the incident. The fact that John gives us both the name of the victim (Malchus), his role (servant of the high priest), and his assailant's name (Peter), facts which the other gospels leave out, is understandable from someone who knew the high priest and who was writing later than the other gospel writers. There was then less need for secrecy about such details, especially that Peter had severed Malchus' ear.

Micklem suggests that the ear was not entirely severed.[12] The accounts tell us it was, and we have no reason to disbelieve them in the light of the fact that three were eyewitnesses. Luke's account is simple, Jesus 'touched his ear and healed him' (22:51). It is unlikely that Luke intended his readers to believe that the ear was restored, or he would have said so more clearly. What Luke is describing is a healing of the wound caused by the amputation.

But the incident obviously served a useful purpose in the early church to stress the non-violent character of Jesus' ministry. Micklem points out that the restoring of Peter's sword to its scabbard is more important than that of the ear to Malchus' head. Luke is particularly eager to illustrate the graciousness of the Lord, here rendering immediate first-aid to the victim of his disciple's indiscretion and thus blessing one of his enemies. Perhaps the greatest miracle in this story is that Peter only severed an ear and did not cleave Malchus' skull. A fatality at that stage would have spelt disaster to the apostolic band, and the removal of its leader, who had been prepared and trained by Jesus for that very role. Just as well Peter's aim was so poor!

Thus the last healing takes place, and one of Jesus' enemies benefits. Within hours the greatest healing of all would release benefits beyond all measure upon mankind.

Chapter
8

Was Jesus Christ a "Superstar"?

What is impossible to God? Not that which is difficult to his power, but that which is contrary to his nature.

Ambrose

Currently it is more fashionable to stress the humanity of Jesus than his deity. So those who react to the 'soft sell' approach, are often forced into an equally unbalanced over-emphasis of Jesus' deity. Both his natures are visible in the New Testament, and they need to be held carefully in balance. Dietrich Bonhoeffer put it well when he said, 'If Jesus Christ is not true God, how could he *help* us? If he is not true man, how could he help *us*?' Lack of interest and concern for the healings of Jesus have contributed to this polarisation. The healings are a demonstration of divine power, which those who stress his humanity, often overlook. Equally, those who stress his deity, do not understand the human aspects of his healing work, and thus minimise his humanity. It was interesting that some of the evangelical critics of the first draft of this book found these human aspects unacceptable. We need to realise that Jesus was limited in certain ways, including that of his healing work. According to Mark 6:5, 6 Jesus couldn't do certain miracles in Nazareth because of unbelief. The Son of God could not bulldoze people to health.

Jesus was truly and fully human. His weakness, vulnerability and frailty are there to be seen in the gospels. This has led one English bishop to speak of God as 'weak as water'. Modern society seeks wealth, education and status for its security. Jesus had none of these. He had no regular income during the three years of his public ministry. He died a pauper's death and was buried in a borrowed tomb. He had no higher education, degrees or earned doctorates. He had no standing army and no weapons to defend himself with. He had a few secret but uncommitted disciples in high places, but otherwise no influential sponsorship. He had no official position in either the synagogue, the state or commerce.

This has led some to present Jesus as a meek and mild character, although even looking at his humanity one wonders how such a distortion could have taken place. The weak attitudes of many to the healings of Jesus has no doubt been a major contribution to this distortion of the truth. Even George Bernard Shaw, who was no friend of the church, rejected such a picture of the Lord. 'It is a snivelling modern invention,' he wrote, 'with no warrant in the Gospels.' When we see Jesus taking authority over demons and commanding them to leave people, calling the dead back to life and exhibiting such a command of situations to earn the admiration of an officer in the Roman army, it is far removed from the sickly and sentimental 'meek and mild' Jesus presented to us in the past.

Jesus' power was 'naked' in the sense that it owed nothing to human accomplishments, which normally embellish the work of great men. It was acquired neither by the pen nor the sword. There wasn't a trace of ruthlessness in it. But the power was there, make no mistake about it. Backs were straightened, wounds instantly healed, demons expelled, fevers rebuked and leprosy shrivelled. Jesus himself attributed it to the Father rather than anything he innately possessed. And it was all backed up with stunning inspiration. Jesus saw through people with X-ray accuracy. He knew what they were thinking. He saw under their guard. He recognised what was the matter with the sick before they had time to tell him. He short-circuited lengthy counselling sessions with 'words of knowledge' which instantly gave the right clues to facilitate the healing.

Everywhere Jesus went he functioned as a healer. There

are forty-one recorded occasions of his healings, but there were many others which are unrecorded, as John points out (20:30). He healed people individually, in pairs and in small and large groups. He healed through touch, prayer, words of authority, spittle and mud. He healed people who touched him without his knowing it, and people at a distance who neither heard him nor saw him. He healed the good and the bad, Jews and Gentiles, the rich and the poor, the strong and the weak. Only stubborn unbelief and self-righteousness seemed to hinder him.

According to the gospel records, Jesus Christ clearly manifested the power of God. This was true in both the tenses of the kingdom in the New Testament – as a present reality seen, heard and experienced in his ministry, and a future hope for the end of the age, equally clearly centred on the person of Christ. Luke more than the other gospel writers emphasises this feature of his ministry. Right from the birth of Christ, 'power was in the air'. It was 'the power of the Most High' which overshadowed the virgin Mary (Lk 1:35); it was 'in the power of the Spirit' that Jesus returned into Galilee (Lk 4:14); it was 'with authority and power' that he commanded the spirits to leave (Lk 4:36; 9:1); and when he healed the sick, Luke tells us that 'the power of the Lord was present to heal' (5:17). In Acts Luke records for us the summary that Peter gives of Jesus' ministry, 'God anointed Jesus of Nazareth with the Holy Spirit and with power . . .' (10:38). The passage goes on to describe, amongst other things, Jesus' healing ministry. There is no doubt that the healings of Jesus were closely connected to the word 'power' which occurs over a hundred times in the New Testament. Jesus was a man of power and he gave the same gift to the church at Pentecost. He promised them 'you shall receive *power* when the Holy Spirit has come upon you' (Acts 1:8).

In all these quotations the word used in the Greek is *dunamis*. It is usually translated 'power', though in Mark and Luke, in an important passage (Mk 5:30; Lk 6:19; 8:46), it has sometimes been translated 'virtue'. The word has overtones of 'ability', and needs to be carefully looked at owing to the malevolent possibilities in the popular use of this word. We shall see that, although at a superficial level there seem to be similarities between Jesus' work and that of the contemporary miracle workers and magicians, at a deeper level his work was very different. This would certainly be true when the word 'power' is applied to his work. There is the classic example in Acts of Simon Magus, who also exercised power, but whose motivation was false. The source of his power was also different. In Acts 8 we are told that he was regarded by the people of Samaria as 'that power of God which is called Great' (v. 10). He had practised magic and amazed everyone. But as soon as he encountered the apostle Peter his true character was revealed and he was called upon to repent. We need to remember that there were many people like Simon Magus operating in the Roman empire in the first century – and they all claimed to have the 'power' to perform miracles.

We need to look critically at some of the translations of *dunamis*, especially as 'mighty works' and 'various miracles' (Acts 2:22; Heb 2:4). *Dunamis* points to new and higher forces which have entered and are at work in this world. There are other words such as *ischus* and *kratos* which are sometimes used; but *dunamis* is the most commonly employed and is used in most of the books of the New Testament with the single and interesting exception of John's gospel. The word 'ability' is not far from the meaning of *dunamis*, although an exact translation is difficult. It is a word which needs to be carefully understood in the context in which it appears and interpreted in the healing ministry of Jesus in the light of the other aspects of those remarkable three years.

It is not uncommon for some of the bad features of 'power' to be carried over uncritically into the modern faith healing movement with sometimes distressing results. Both the love of power for its own sake and the misuse of it are dangerous. These are ever-present temptations, particularly in healing ministries, and those involved in them need to watch very carefully that they do not fall for them.

Power in the Old and New Testaments

In the Old Testament the two most commonly used Hebrew words are *yad* and *koach*. God's power is manifested chiefly in nature and history. God is revealed as one who influences not only Israel, but all the nations of the world who are like 'a drop in a bucket' (Isa 40:15). Biblical revelation did not come from the evolution of ideas. It is not ideological. It is not to do with human theories. It stands or falls on actual historical events. These happenings are seen as manifestations of the power of God. For example, the only explanation of the remarkable deliverance of God's people from Egypt and the Red Sea is the actual direct intervention of God. The power of God needs, therefore, to be seen in terms of concrete events in history.

The same understanding of the nature of the power of God is transferred to the New Testament. There too the gospel writers appeal to concrete manifestations of power. In the first instance, there are miracles and healings. But the greatest manifestation of all is the resurrection of Jesus Christ from the dead. This is the supreme act of power, which can only be matched by the events at the end of the age, when 'the Son of Man comes on the clouds of heaven with *power* and great glory' (Mt 24:30) and when we shall see, in the words of Jesus, 'the Son of Man seated at the right hand of *Power*' (Mt 26:64).

The word *dunamis* is a key word in our quest to understand the healings of Jesus. The Hebrew mind was not so much concerned about the being of God as his activity. The Old Testament is not primarily interested in metaphysical questions about who God is. Its overwhelming testimony is to the decisive acts of God in the personal lives of people. Thus power tends to be seen in dynamic rather than static terms. According to Alan Richardson, '*Dunamis* means both latent capability of action and also power in action; it represents the Being of God in his dynamic aspect, that is the only aspect in which we can know him.'[1] Paul in Romans 1:20 talks of God's 'eternal power and deity'. And Jesus opened wide the doors of faith when he said 'With men it is impossible, but not with God; for all things are possible (*panta dunata*) with God' Mk 10:27).

In the biblical sense all true *dunamis* is derived from God and delegated to us by him. There are other sources of power, for example that employed by Simon Magus. But the power of God is always greater. Jesus' ability to heal the sick is directly attributed to his possession of this power of God. In Luke 5:17 we read, 'and the power of the Lord was with him to heal'. In fact as Alan Richardson points out, 'all the events in history to which the New Testament bears witness can be seen to be related to the effectual working of the *dunamis* of God'.[2]

Some have distinguished sharply between the words 'power' (*dunamis*) and 'authority' (*exousia*). They come closely together in Acts 1:7 and 8. Jesus speaks of the times and seasons which have been fixed by the Father's authority (*exousia*). He then goes on to tell the disciples what they were to expect – 'you shall receive power (*dunamis*) when the Holy Spirit has come upon you'. Here and elsewhere in the New Testament the words are different, though in English (and in some older translations) they overlap in that the word 'power' can be substituted for the word 'authority'. Some, in distinguishing between these two words, have forced them wider apart than they should.

There is a good example of these two important notions coming together in the story in Luke 7:1–10 of the healing of the centurion's slave. The faith that the centurion had in the *power* of God to heal his sick slave was based on his respect for the *authority* that Jesus had. Because he understood and accepted the nature of *authority* he could also perceive where the *power* came from to heal his slave. 'Say the word, and let my servant be healed' he declared. Thus 'power' and 'authority', though different words, have a vital connection, for they represent the same general meaning. God's power is one thing, the right to use it and the way it should be used is something else. In the incarnation the Son of God laid aside his divine rights, and supremely on the cross refused to exercise power to save himself. To have done so would have been to turn against the very authority upon which that power stands or falls.

To say this is only to declare what is obvious throughout the New Testament. All forms of supernatural power, even satanic, derive their authority from God. In Ephesians, Christ is declared to be 'far above all rule and authority and power and dominion and above every name that is named' (Eph 1:21). The same idea of superiority comes in Colossians 1:16; 1 Corinthians 8:5, 6 and Romans 8:35–39. Demons are under the authority of Jesus Christ, and in his name, under that of his disciples. The two words come together in Luke 10:19, when Jesus said to the seventy, 'I have given you *authority* to tread upon serpents and scorpions, and over all the *power* of the enemy; and nothing shall hurt you.' There is no question whatsoever about it. The kingdom of God has come and all demonic forces have to bow to the name of Jesus Christ.

It is Luke who develops the theme of 'power' most fully in his gospel and in the Acts of the Apostles. In fact it would seem to be the main subject running through both these pieces of writing. He is concerned to show that Jesus' ministry was a powerful one, that he amazed people with the signs and wonders that he performed, and that he quickly got his disciples in on the act by sending out first the twelve (Lk 9:1ff) and then the seventy (Lk 10:1ff). We need to notice that Jesus did not go with them. They were now on their own, but similarly commissioned 'to preach the kingdom of God and heal' (Lk 9:2). It is even more specific in Lk 10:1 that they were sent on 'ahead of him'. It is Luke too who most clearly specifies the build-up to Pentecost and the purpose of the event, which was that his disciples would be 'clothed with power from on high' (24:49) and that they would receive power when the Holy Spirit came upon them (Acts 1:8). From the ascension onwards they would be even more 'on their own'. But Christ's work would carry on through them and spread to the whole world. In Acts Luke shows how the ministry of Jesus, not least his healing ministry, continued through the work of the disciples both within the church and outside it.

This power, to which the gospel writers give witness, was linked closely with the key teaching about the kingdom of God. Alan Richardson writes 'the Kingdom of God is an irresistible *dunamis* silently at work in the world'.[3] I like his use of the word 'silently', but we need to remember that the Holy Spirit does not always work that way. Sometimes it can be a noisy affair. When Jesus delivered some people from evil spirits the noise was heard all over town. One hardly imagines Jesus whispering the words, 'Lazarus come forth'!

The writer of the epistle to the Hebrews describes Christians as those who 'have become partakers of the Holy Spirit, and have tasted the goodness of the word of God and the powers of the age to come' (6:4–5). That was true of the earliest disciples of Christ. For starters they had an experience of the power of God which was preparatory to the main course which was yet to come. The first and most brilliant model had been the ministry of our Lord Jesus Christ. They were convinced that their Lord and Master wanted them to go in the power of the same Spirit and do the same work everywhere they went. The Acts of the Apostles provides evidence that this is exactly what they did after Pentecost.

The most famous passage in which 'kingdom' and 'power' are united is the Lord's prayer (Mt 6:13, see margin). Here we have 'kingdom', 'power' and 'glory' attributed to God. As we shall see, the word 'glory' has a special significance in the gospel of John. A less famous instance is in 1 Corinthians 4:20, 'For the kingdom of God does not consist in talk but in power.' Here Paul is referring to his wordy critics who were great talkers, and one assumes, interested in tittle-tattle and the allurements of gossip, which seem to have been rife in the church in Corinth. But Paul in his defence juxtaposes 'kingdom' and 'power' in a significant way. We find the same combination of words in Revelation 12:10 where the reference is to 'the salvation and the power and the kingdom of our God'.

In the New Testament, miracles (*dunameis*) are manifestations of God's *dunamis*. We have already pointed out that both words are absent from John's gospel. The word 'glory' (*doxa*) is the equivalent in John's gospel. This comes out clearly in John 2:11, 'This, the first of his signs, Jesus did at Cana in Galilee and manifested his *glory*'. Here we could easily substitute the word 'power' for 'glory', and Luke almost certainly would have done so. It is interesting to notice that John adds the words, 'and his disciples believed in him', reiterating the point Luke constantly makes that signs and wonders encourage faith. But John is not the only author in the New Testament who links 'glory' with 'power'. We have already seen it in the doxology that ends the Lord's prayer (Mt 6:13 mg). Paul also links it in Romans 6:4 when he writes that 'Christ was raised from the dead 'by the glory of the Father'. So we see in the New Testament an interesting interchange of words and ideas; 'wisdom' (*sophia*), 'spirit' (*pneuma*), 'kingdom' (*basileia*), 'grace' (*charis*), and 'glory' (*doxa*). Richardson writes of these words, 'they are all like *dunamis* agents or modes or expressions or instruments or even results of the dynamic activity of God'.[4]

The code of the kingdom

It is pretty obvious that naked power is both a temptation to those who desire it and a manifest danger to those who are the victims of its misuse. Count Leo Tolstoy wrote about power that in order to obtain and hold it 'man must love it'. He goes on, 'the effort to get it is not likely to be coupled with goodness, but with the opposite qualities of pride, craft and cruelty'. The whole of the Bible and, in fact, all human history, affirms this. Jesus himself died in the crossfire of human greed for power and the unwillingness to surrender it to anyone. Herod, Pilate, the people and the Sanhedrin were all like puppets manipulated by obsession for power. The greater the power, the more dangerous the abuse.

Jesus was also tempted to abuse the power he had. It was an

important aspect of his temptations in the wilderness. If he had not had the power, for example, to turn stones into bread, it would not have been a temptation for him to do it. The final act of obedience, his death on the cross, was a clear surrender of power in an act of obedience. When we understand the tension that Jesus experienced during his earthly ministry, we can begin to see the way he overcame this temptation. The kingdom was in code language, and only those who knew the code could understand the kingdom and all that goes with it.

This may explain the seeming contradiction between Jesus' open ministry of signs and wonders and his flat refusal to produce signs for the curious or to prove his messiahship, and also the fact that there were occasions when Jesus sent his disciples out to proclaim the gospel of the kingdom from the rooftops, whereas on other occasions he told some of them to go and tell no one. Jesus spoke (e.g. the parables), and acted (e.g. the miracles) in a kind of code language. Some knew the code and some didn't. The only way the code could be cracked was through repentance and faith. But even the disciples, after several years of close fellowship with Jesus, did not understand it until much later – hence the remarkable question put to Christ by some of them just before Pentecost, 'will you at this time restore the kingdom to Israel?' (Acts 1:6). This shows that even after three years of closely following Christ they still did not properly understand the kingdom.

The classic statement about the secret code comes in Mark 4:10–12. Jesus had just been teaching his disciples and a crowd of people. In the privacy of the disciples' company he opens up the subject. 'To you', he said, 'has been given the secret of the kingdom of God, but for the outside everything is in parables'. Only certain people will grasp what the kingdom is all about. Jesus travelled incognito through life. Paul brings this out in 2 Corinthians 13:4, Jesus 'was crucified in weakness, but lives by the power of God'. The 'weakness' (*astheneia*) of Christ hides the *dunamis* of God. Paul also knew this secret in his personal life. Thus in the previous chapter his 'thorn in the flesh' was to teach him that God's power 'is made perfect in weakness' (2 Cor 12:9). Paul's apparent 'weakness' was so effective as a 'veil' that those whom he called 'superlative apostles' in Corinth could not properly evaluate his ministry.

So Jesus' 'weakness' was a secret code which only a handful understood. 'Can anything good come out of Nazareth?' some critically said of Jesus (Jn 1:46). 'Is not this Joseph's son?' they said on another occasion (Lk 4:22). Matthew tells us that Jesus could do no mighty work in Nazareth 'because of their unbelief' (Mt 13:58). The veil of the 'flesh' hid the glory of God from the prying eyes of those who did not mean business. In Jesus' case a part of the veil was his humble origins and lack of status in the sight of men. Thus Jesus himself was part of that hidden code. The only way to crack it was to recognise him as Lord.

Although the New Testament was written that men might believe, it is clear in both the gospels and the epistles that the most precious gifts of God lie hidden until they are found, and that they are not discovered by the normal intellectual processes of reason and logic. This is especially true of the kingdom of God. According to the parables it is like leaven which is hidden in the dough (Mt 13:33), treasure hidden in a field (Mt 13:44), and seed hidden in the ground (Mk 4:26–29). Jesus rejoiced that the kingdom had been hidden from the wise and understanding and only revealed to babes (Mt 11:25, Lk 10:21). This is also true of wisdom (*sophia*), which Paul describes as 'secret and hidden' and only revealed 'through the Spirit' (1 Cor 2:7, 10), and of glory (*doxa*) which is referred to as both seen and hidden, both revealed and to be revealed (see 1 Cor 2:8; Rom 8:18; 1 Peter 5:1).

In John's gospel there is a change of emphasis. The other gospels contrast the enlightened and unenlightened disciples – particularly before and after the resurrection and ascension. But in John's gospel it is between the disciples who understand and the world that doesn't. Judas (one of the other disciples, not Judas Iscariot) asks the question bluntly, 'how is it that you will manifest yourself to us, and not to the world?' (Jn 14:22). To him everything is open and plain, though not all believe and accept what they see and hear. John concentrates on the word 'glory', and a summary of his gospel could well be the words 'we beheld his glory' from the famous prologue (1:14). The centrality of the cross is even more explicit in John than in the synoptics.

Testimony of power

For the early Christians one of the clearest signs that Jesus Christ was the Messiah of God was the power revealed through his healing miracles. Alan Richardson rejects Bultmann's argument which compares the miracle stories with Greek wonder-workers. This he says 'is entirely false to the theological stand-point of the New Testament which sees in the miracles of the Lord a revelation of the power and of the saving purpose of God'.[5] They are not a secondary stratum. He goes on, 'they cannot be understood apart from the teaching of the early church as a whole, of which they are a characteristic vehicle'.

Peter at Pentecost said of Jesus Christ that he was 'a man attested to you by God with mighty works and wonders and signs which God did through him in your midst, as you yourselves know' (Acts 2:22). One cannot, if one is fair to the gospels, miss the point that they are concerned with a person who eminently and significantly manifested the power and grace of God. Luke tells us that 'all the crowd sought to touch him, for power (*dunamis*) came forth from him and healed them all' (Lk 6:19). The hidden and secret factor was one thing. The unmistakable evidence of the power of God in the lives of countless witnesses, most of whom would have lived for several years after the death of Jesus, was something else.

However, we must not detach the miracles from their theological basis. To do so is to be unfaithful to those who have recorded the stories. The significance of what Jesus did can only be fully understood in the light of the person who did them. There is an important association in the words of Christ in Mark 12:24, 'Is not this why you are wrong, that you know

neither the scriptures nor the power of God?' We must not, in
our fear of the misuse of power, run away from the clear
importance attached in the New Testament to Christ as the
'man of power'.

The early Christians claimed to possess that same power
which Christ had manifested, particularly in his healing work.
Jesus passed on to the twelve and then to an increasingly wide
band of disciples the same gifts of the Holy Spirit. For the
Christian community this power was the ground of its life and
its faith. The miracles were not recorded solely to excite
people, but were an essential part of the gospel preaching of
which the true purpose was to awaken faith in the saving
revelation of God's power towards those that believe.

The Lord's prayer ends with the words 'thine is the kingdom, the power and the glory'. We have seen already how
closely related these words are in the New Testament. In the
synoptics the emphasis is on 'kingdom' and 'power'; but this
imbalance is redressed in John's gospel where the emphasis is
on 'glory'. We have noticed how 'glory' is John's word for
'power', and the word *dunamis* does not occur in the fourth
gospel. It would seem that to remove 'power' from the
kingdom is to emasculate it. It is axiomatic in the New
Testament that where the kingdom of God is, there will also
be found the power of God, whether that power is manifested
in healing miracles or the blood and sweat of Calvary.

But to remove the word 'glory' from the kingdom is to set it
at risk, for the surest safeguard against the abuse of power is
found in this very word, seen so often in John's gospel.
Healings are for God's glory not man's. This should save us
from the perverted kind of ministry so common in Jesus' day,
which he himself repudiated. There is a ministry which
attracts people to a 'star' on a platform, and which glorifies
that person rather than the Lord. But Jesus himself ran away
from all such forms of self-adulation. He didn't have a mailing
list of supporters. He didn't advertise his meetings and he
usually discouraged those whom he healed from talking about
it to others. Only once does he speak about his own miracles
and that was to encourage John the Baptist when he was

imprisoned by Herod. It is a mistake to ignore the example of Christ, as the true man of power, yet who was never the 'Superstar', but we should never detach the miracles from the context in which they can alone be properly understood. If we do we shall gravely distort them and create an entirely false spirituality.

Chapter
9

Signs and Wonders

The world will never starve for want of wonders, but
only for want of wonder.

G. K. Chesterton

I have not called this chapter 'miracles' but 'signs and wonders' for a number of reasons. For one thing the normal
Greek word for 'miracles' is *thauma*, and it is never used in the
New Testament to describe an event, only the wonder and
admiration of people responding to an event. There are two
words which are sometimes translated 'miracle' in the English
translations, *dunamis* and *semeion*, literally 'an act of power'
and 'a sign'. For example in 1 Corinthians 12:10 the word used
to describe 'working of miracles' is *dunamis*. In the GNB
there are a number of references in John's gospel to the word
'miracle', but it is always a translation of the word *semeion*
(e.g. Jn 2:11; 2:23; 3:2 etc). The RSV usually translates this
word 'sign'. The NIV uses the phrase 'miraculous signs' in an
attempt to preserve both aspects. In the light of the fact that
thauma is never used to describe the action of God by any of
the New Testament writers we should be cautious about using
the word 'miracle' even though in this chapter and elsewhere
it is frequently mentioned. The word is in such common use it
is impossible to avoid it, but we should take care to know what
we are talking about when we do.

Hans Küng describes the word 'miracle' as 'almost as vague
as "revolution"'.[1] Today it is used freely by some to describe
man's scientific or physical achievements. An even more
modern word used in the same context is 'magic'. Goethe
called the miracle 'the dearest child of faith'. But that is

frankly condescending. Although the use of the word is unavoidable, we must not allow the word to be hijacked by the credulous, and thus distorted or even de-christianised. Both those who claim too much and those who deny altogether the reality of miracles obscure the subject by their stances.

The Greek word *thauma* was used from the time of Homer to describe 'miracles'. But, as we have observed, it is not used in the New Testament to describe the signs and wonders done by Jesus and his disciples. Nor does Jerome use the word *miraculum* in the Vulgate. It is important when we examine the healing ministry of Jesus Christ to notice how the gospel writers make plain that Jesus' ministry owes nothing to the miracle workers who were his contemporaries. He was in a different league. There have always been naive people ready to believe almost anything. Jesus was not a magician. For him miracles were always means not ends in themselves. So to use the word 'miracle' without any qualification as a way of describing what Jesus did would be to place him on a par with other 'miracle workers' and so to distort his personality and his work. It is this very link that the gospel writers dissociate themselves from. But Bultmann does make that very association. The miracles according to him were later additions patterned on the work of these people. His view has been criticised by Alan Richardson in his book *Miracle stories of the gospel*.[2]

The New Testament uses several words to describe what we call 'miracles' – wonders, signs, mighty works, and works. A study of these words and their meaning and significance is in a separate appendix (page 179).

Signs and wonders: an historical perspective

It is often assumed that miracles first became a problem with the development of the scientific view of man and creation. This, as we shall see, is a mistake and needs to be corrected. On the other hand, primitive man saw miracles in everything.

To him all things were equally wonderful, and many things that for us would have a perfectly natural explanation were marvelled at by the primitive who had no scientific knowledge as a yardstick to judge what he was experiencing. Mensching writes, 'in the primitive milieu the natural is wonderful and the wonderful natural'.[3]

Miracles figure quite prominently in the Old Testament, usually associated with outstanding leaders like Moses, Elijah and Elisha. But they seem to diminish during and after the period of the exile and become less associated with the prophetic ministry than they were in the earlier period. We need, however, to remember that it was Ezekiel who wrote of the false shepherds, 'the sick you have not healed' (34:4). John the Baptist, described by the Lord Jesus Christ as the greatest of those 'born of women' up to that time (Mt 11:11), never healed the sick or performed signs and wonders so far as we know. During the New Testament period the countries fringing the Mediterranean were the happy hunting ground of numerous miracle workers, magicians, astrologers, sorcerers, prophets and so on. The occult was rife. Belief in miracles flourished during this period. At famous sites like Athens, Ephesus, Pergamum and Cos stood temples and shrines where people could go, as they do today to Lourdes and Fatima, to receive healing. Healing gurus abounded. We know about Simon Magus from Acts 8:18–24. Yet he was not by any means the only one who was amazing people with his magic. Famous names include Apollonius of Tyana, Alexander of Abonouteichos and even some of the Roman emperors.

Miracles in other religions

The founders of many of the world's religions also found miracles a problem and rejected them. Confucius in China refused to accept miracles at all. Buddha was only interested in miracles to help man understand his inner self. The doctrine of the Buddha was regarded as the miracle. Mohammed totally denied miracles. For him there was only one miracle and that was the Koran. He had no desire to do miracles, in this he displayed a commendable modesty. All the world's religions, other than Christianity and Judaism, have rejected the place of miracles in their essential teaching. Their founders never claimed any miracles for themselves; nor were their lives dependent upon them.

But we should notice that these founders of world religions were not protesting *scientifically* against miracles, for their world had no such criteria to judge the miraculous. As Loos puts it 'for them miracles belonged to the lower regions and so were in conflict with the higher spiritual spheres of their doctrines'.[4] Unlike our Lord Jesus Christ, these religious teachers did not accept man in his totality. They did not teach the need for the 'redemption of the body'. In pursuit of the spiritual, like the later Gnostic heretics, they tended to denigrate the human body. They, therefore, were comparatively indifferent to human sickness. It was not so much whether miracles could happen, but rather whether they were really necessary.

Another interesting observation is the way in which myths and legendary stories have grown up around the lives of these founders and other great religious leaders. This goes to show that even if the founders themselves rejected miracles, their followers sometimes didn't. We could mention for example the legends about the birth of Buddha and Mohammed, and the story of Mohammed splitting the moon in two when the inhabitants of Mecca prayed for a sign. The popularisers of religions have often taken this course and Christianity itself has not escaped such treatment. Claims of spectacular miracles are part of the folklore of Christianity, and account at least partly for the Reformers' scepticism about them. They were reacting against the scandalous behaviour of those who exploited the credulity of the crowds and, often for financial benefit, made claim to be the 'workers of miracles'. Thus the relics of the saints were said to possess healing powers and healing shrines sprang up all over western Europe. The phenomena of Lourdes, Fatima and other more recent healing centres need to be considered critically in the light of this factor. People love miracles. They are comforting and reassuring. They seem to bring God nearer.

However, the miracles of Jesus are in a different category. They were spontaneous, not stage-managed. Jesus never held a healing service as such. He never founded a healing shrine. Unfortunately magicians and charlatans, making their spurious claims, have abounded throughout the pages of history. Perhaps it was with this in mind that Confucius, Buddha and Mohammed turned their backs resolutely on all miracles.

But Jesus didn't. In this he again demonstrated the uniqueness of his claims to being the Son of God. Christianity is alone amongst the world's religions in claiming to possess by the grace of God and the power of the Holy Spirit the ability to heal the sick and do miracles. It is true that the popularisers of other religions perform miracles too, though one must ask serious questions about where they obtain the power to do them. But the Christian claim to possess the power to heal the sick rests in the fact that Christ not only healed the sick himself, but commissioned his disciples to do it. And even if some Christians have taken it down the wrong track, the evidence for all to see is that the ministry of divine healing has never been absent from the church for very long. We, in the twentieth century, have witnessed the greatest developments of this ministry since the first century.

The birth of scepticism

To the founders of the great world religions, miracles were irrelevant. They had no place for them in their systems. We need, now, to look at another influence which centuries later was to challenge the whole approach of the church to belief in miracles and divine healing.

There are interesting parallels between the classical approach of the Greeks and Romans and later rationalism and humanism. The two are, in any case, closely related to each other, since humanism derives its inspiration from the

Greeks and Romans. One parallel was the antagonism that existed between popular credulity which accepted miracles and the sophisticated philosophies which didn't. Claims of miracles abounded in the Graeco-Roman world around the first century. Healers operated, as we have already noticed, in many parts of the Roman empire. Perhaps the most famous of all statements denying miracles is that of Cicero, who died only about forty years before the birth of Jesus Christ. This is what he wrote:

> For nothing can happen without cause; nothing happens that cannot happen, and when what was capable of happening has happened, it may not be interpreted as a miracle. Consequently there are no miracles . . . we, therefore, draw this conclusion: what was incapable of happening never happened, and what was capable of happening is not a miracle.[5]

Here is a clear and unequivocal statement by a man who is locking the Creator out of his creation. In simple words we are face to face with the atheistic mind. Here is the humanist who says 'man is the measure of all things'. Cicero's brilliance was matched by many others during this period who ridiculed belief in miracles. We therefore find at an early period an assault on the miraculous which was by the eighteenth and nineteenth centuries to become a crusade. Had it succeeded, it would have effectively wiped Christianity from the face of Europe. As time went on it was not only the claims of current miracles which came under attack, but eventually the miracles of Jesus were disputed and rejected by some within as well as outside the church. This has led some to reject the doctrine of the incarnation as well as the miracles which the evangelists claimed Jesus Christ performed.

The assault of rationalism

The first to mount this campaign was Spinoza (1632–1677) who had been deeply influenced by the new scientific approach to philosophy in his day. According to Spinoza God is the cause of everything and he acts in accordance with strict laws. His system of thought effectively ruled out all miracles. Here the seeds of Cicero's approach are bearing fruit. Spinoza was the first to successfully undermine the church's confidence in the miraculous.

In England during the eighteenth century the campaign was carried on by the Deists such as Conyers Middleton and Edward Gibbon. Others like Thomas Chubb (1679–1746), Henry St John Bolingbroke (1678–1751) and Thomas Hobbes (1588–1679) attacked the miracles of the Bible. Bolingbroke, for example, argued that if the miracles of the Old Testament had really happened it would be the greatest miracle of all that such a religion had not been accepted immediately by the entire world. Thomas Hobbes declared himself to be against all belief in miracles.

Perhaps the strongest voice was that of the sceptic David Hume (1711–1776). In an essay on miracles in 1748 he refers to them as 'a violation of the laws of nature', which he regarded as firm and unalterable. Another opponent of miracles was Thomas Woolston (1670–1731) who was imprisoned in 1729 because of his book *Discourses on the Miracles of our Saviour*, which was considered distasteful. He refused to accept the literal interpretation of Jesus' miracles.

What was a strong stream in Britain soon became a flood in France and Germany. Rationalism ruled supreme and the traditional authority of the church was overthrown. The French Revolution was to cast its shadow over the next two hundred years of European history. The church never recovered its ground. Reason was considered the sole source of human enlightenment.

In the nineteenth century it was German theology which dominated the scene. Here there is a gradual but seemingly relentless shifting of ground – a movement which takes us further and further from faith in miracles. H. E. G. Paulus (1761–1851) called for a separation of the facts as they were and the opinions which the evangelists had about them. F. D. Schleiermacher (1768–1834) agreed that in the gospels miracles played an important part. But he saw the miracles as human actions which find their point of departure in moral motives. He preferred to think of the exorcisms as relief of mental illness. We see here the continuing use of rationalistic techniques – so far on a moderate scale. The stream is gathering momentum. D. F. Strauss (1808–1874) tried to apply Hegelian philosophical principles to the gospels. He regarded supernaturalism as old-fashioned. This led him along a new pathway with mythical explanations of the miracles. Thus the foundations were being laid for the demythologising of the gospels. Strauss saw 'eternal truths' in the events without feeling he needed to answer the question 'did they actually happen?'

By the beginning of the twentieth century a furious battle was being waged on many fronts and in many parts of the world around the issue of miracles. Faith and science were being increasingly polarised into two camps – 'believers' and 'unbelievers'. The First Vatican Council was at least in part called to defend the Roman Catholic Church from this liberal assault. The Fundamentalist battle in the twentieth century was fought on the same issue. Adolf von Harnack also displayed a coldness towards miracles. He asserted that miracles never happen but inexplicable things do! As Loos puts it 'he recognises the *mirabile* but not the *miraculum*'.[6] Harnack accepted miracles when there was a natural explanation, but not when this was not present. 'The question of the meaning of the miracle stories fades into insignificance compared with all the beauty of the Gospels',[7] he wrote, which shows on which side his bread was buttered.

Another development, which should not surprise us, was the attempt to explain the healings of Jesus in psychological terms. This arose in the wake of the growing interest in psychology in the early part of the twentieth century. The most famous of those who trod this pathway was E. R. Micklem who wrote a book called *Miracles and the New Psychology* published in 1922.[8] He worked out his propositions on the basis that Jesus had a great understanding of human character, and was a remarkably sympathetic man who had an easy empathy with people. Micklem's approach was followed by others, such as Leslie Weatherhead, who popularised it. He, together with others, attempted in the twentieth century to give natural explanations for the miracle stories. Dr Martyn Lloyd-Jones, for many years minister of Westminster Chapel in London and a man who wielded considerable influence in the evangelical world during the mid-century, waged a ceaseless battle against these attempts to 'explain away' miracles.

But the most influential development during the twentieth century has undoubtedly been the so-called *Formgeschichte* method, or 'form criticism', an attempt to look at the miracles from a completely new angle. It is this attempt to get behind the written sources that will always be associated with the name of its foremost exponent, Rudolf Bultmann (1884–1976). He believed that most of the accounts of miracles in the gospels are the distillation of legends and must be related to the Hellenistic miracles which were commonly being claimed by Jesus' contemporaries. For him miracles in the New Testament were 'wonders'. He writes,

> they are not works of Christ in so far as we understand by the work of Christ the work of redemption. Consequently in so far as they are events from the past, they must be radically exposed to criticism and it must be argued with the greatest severity that the Christian faith has absolutely no interest in proving the possibility or reality of the miracles of Jesus as events from the past, and that this would on the contrary merely be an error. If Christ stands before us as the Christ preached to us, then the miracles of Christ can only enter into consideration in so far as they form part of the preaching of Christ, that is to say as testimony.[9]

For Bultmann the miracles of Jesus prove that miracles are not suitable for confirming faith. He sees the imperative need to strip the New Testament of the cloak of myths.

It is important that we see the issue as a wider one than the fact or otherwise of miracles. To stop merely at miracles is to stall on the 'wonders' and never to get to the 'signs' without which the 'wonders' have no ultimate meaning. As we have seen the New Testament never does this. There are signs, but never wonders without signs except in so far as they describe the reaction of the spectators. Even if we don't agree with miracles as such, we can still address ourselves to the question, 'Why did the gospel writers include so many alleged miracles in their narratives?' What was it all meant to achieve? We are not dealing with a few scattered and unrelated incidents, which we could summarily dismiss as being of trivial significance. We are handling a high proportion of the narrative of the gospels.

The defenders of the faith

Throughout all the upheavals of the last few hundred years, during the slow but sure advance of science and scientific determinism, there has always existed in the church those whose attitude to miracles in general and to the healings of Jesus in particular has been very different. The church has never lacked those who have believed in the reliability of the stories in the gospels and those who have believed in the continuing miraculous flow of grace and power from God. Loos suggests that there is a 'faith position' upon which he himself feels it is right to stand. He writes, 'whoever believes that the God of Israel sent His Son Jesus Christ the Lord and Saviour of the world, will, on the grounds of this belief and profession, understand and interpret the miracles of the New Testament in a certain way'.[10] He sees it as part of the 'credo'.

Alan Richardson makes the same point when he says that the response to the question concerning the historicity of miracles,

is always a personal answer. It is not the judgment of an historian qua scientific investigator, or the verdict of a school of theologians, or the pronouncement of an

authoritative council of churchmen. The present writer
can do no more than testify to his conviction that in Christ
the power of God was indeed revealed: the miracles
did happen.[11]

I too take this faith position, which for me is not blind or
irrational. I stand firmly on it, with my eyes wide open. I am
not threatened by theological reflections or reasonable in-
vestigations into the meaning of miracles. Some keep their
eyes firmly closed in case, perhaps, they might be proved
wrong. If that is indeed their attitude, then their faith is
unreal.

When my faith in miracles, acquired from childhood from
assumptions planted in me by simple believers, was first
threatened, and I began to realise that there were theologians
and church teachers who doubted and even denied them, I
was initially as threatened as a child who is told that there is no
such person as Father Christmas and that there aren't any
fairies at the bottom of the garden. The world of fantasy and
magic disappears into thin air like a burst bubble. That kind of
unreality has to go anyway. I remember the feeling of pain
when doubts began to arise in my mind about the healing
miracles of Jesus. Then one Sunday morning at Cambridge I
heard a sermon on the text, 'God did not give us a spirit of
timidity but a spirit of power and love and self-control' (2 Tim
1:7). As a result my fears evaporated not my faith. I could
trust God completely. I could rely on him enough to keep my
eyes wide open. I could look miracles in the face. If they were
myths and fables, then the sooner I saw this the better. If they
were well-established facts, then I could trust God to make it
plain to me.

We now need to see the movements of opinions as they
have unfolded in church history. Thomas Aquinas subjected
miracles to considerable study and comment. He distinguished between the *mirabile* and the *miraculum*. *Mirabile*
occurs when the effects are clear but the cause obscure. He
gives the example of the eclipse of the sun. One person, who is
unscientific, marvels at it because he does not know the cause,

but the astronomer who does know it does not marvel in the same way. But *miraculum* is something which everyone marvels at because no one knows the cause except God himself. He spoke of miracles 'transcending the powers of nature'. If God intervenes directly we have an absolute miracle.

Augustine, however, had taken a rather different line in his defence of miracles. He saw God *in* nature rather than outside it and intervening whenever a miracle was purposed. He argued for the absolute freedom that God has within his own creation. 'How can anything be against nature that happens by the will of God', he writes, 'since the will of so great a Maker is the nature of every made thing? A miracle therefore does not happen against nature, but against nature as it is known. Who, now, shall count the multitude of miracles preserved in the history of peoples?'[12] For Augustine, then, the laws of nature are simply a further expression of the will of God. He 'wrote' the laws and he has the absolute right to ignore them, repeal them, or suspend them whenever and wherever he likes.

It is also interesting to note that one of the canons of the Vatican Council of 1870 anathematised those who reject miracles. 'If anyone says that no miracles can happen – or that miracles never can be known for certain, or that as a result the divine origin of the Christian religion cannot be definitely proved, he shall be excommunicated.' Strong medicine indeed!

The Reformers took another line. Luther and Calvin discussed miracles in a practical theological framework not from the point of view of theoretical philosophy as did Augustine and Thomas Aquinas. Thus Calvin discussed the sun miracles in Joshua 10 and 2 Kings 20 as revealing that the normal is not a 'blind impulse' of nature. Increasingly, therefore, miracles were being seen as acts of God transcending the powers of nature.

A fine and spirited defence of the faith came from the pen of the Scottish theologian, D. S. Cairns. His book is called *The faith that rebels* and was published in 1928. He saw the malady of his time as,

our contracted thoughts of God. We think too narrowly
and meanly of His Power, His Love and His Freedom to
help men. That is what the 'miracles' of Jesus and His
teaching about Faith mean. That God is more near, more
real and mighty, more full of love and more ready to help
every one of us than any one of us realises, that is their
underlying message.[13]

He writes of our fears of the words of Christ, our minimising
of them and our toning them down. It never occurred to Jesus
Christ that men would make too much of his words. His one
fear was that men would believe too little, which was where
his disciples were often at.

Karl Barth (1886–1968) saw miracles principally in terms of
revelation. He rejected the popular distinction of the school-
men between the ordinary and extraordinary power of God,
'Miracle is not the proof of a special divine omnipotence. It is
a special proof of the one divine omnipotence.'[14] He would
want to eliminate the element of chance as being our assessment of the situation rather than the truth. He sees the
miracles as part of the 'divine shaping and planning, to which
our concepts of planning are simply not equal'.

In the early part of this century there was much controversy
on both sides of the Atlantic when the Pentecostal churches
emerged. They have always had a strong belief in the miraculous and the manifestation of the gifts of the Holy Spirit as a
normal part of church life. In the 1920s in the United States
this controversy was largely eclipsed by the arrival on the
scene of 'Fundamentalism'. The scholar B. B. Warfield was
one of those who contended for the faith on both fronts. As an
Evangelical he rejected liberal theology. As a dispensational-
ist he rebutted the Pentecostals. The gifts of the Spirit and the
miraculous were only for the first century, he argued. The
Warfield thesis is still believed by many Fundamentalists in
the United States, but its influence is waning in most other
parts of the world. The claims for miracles by Pentecostals
meant that Evangelicals had to find some explanation. They
often resorted to asserting that modern so-called miracles

were counterfeit. In Germany the Berlin Declaration of 1907 actually used the term 'counterfeit' to apply to all Pentecostals, who were also designated 'agents of the devil'. The Declaration is still accepted by parts of the German Lutheran Church.

Defining miracles

Many attempts have been made to define miracles and we have already referred to some of these. C. S. Lewis in his book *Miracles* defined them as 'an interference with Nature by supernatural power. Unless there exists, in addition to nature, something else which we may call the supernatural, there can be no miracles. Some people believe that nothing exists except Nature'.[15] This definition has much to commend it since it incorporates the 'faith position'. To accept miracles you have first to accept an independent volitional force which is superior to the natural and is able to control it and bend it to its wishes. You need, in other words, faith in God himself. But C. S. Lewis' use of the word 'supernatural' would be unacceptable to many today. One would need to sharpen up this definition by teasing out the relationship between the natural and the divine. Augustine's view is helpful here. He does not see God 'outside' but working ceaselessly inside his creation. It is not good to make too sharp a distinction between God and nature which the use of the word 'supernatural' tends to do. But we must not press the relationship too close together and thereby become pantheists.

Loos gives us some useful guiding principles:[16]

1. They are a form of divine revelation.
2. They can be observed by anyone, but they can be understood only by faith.
3. They are events which occur *supra et contra naturam* when no natural explanation can be given.
4. They always have meaning for the people concerned and for the whole of mankind.
5. They are manifestations of God's freedom, power and

love. God has ordained order for his creation, but he is
free himself and not bound to that order.

He then goes on to define a miracle as

a direct act of God in which He reveals to mankind, with an
intention, a new observable reality, which can only be fully
understood by faith. In this new reality God proclaims,
outside and against the unknown laws of order and regular-
ity in nature, His freedom, power and love.[17]

We might be defeating the object of miracles by trying to
define them. Like God himself they are beyond absolute
definition. We are using rational techniques in an area where
faith and trust should be the ruling principles. We need to be
prepared to be called 'obscurantist' in our affirmation that
there is a sufficient degree of the divine in miracles to make us
wary of tying the whole subject neatly up in rational parcels.
We shall always find a part that does not properly fit because
the divine defies definition. We are on holy ground so we need
to tread carefully.

It seems that there are two errors which we need to avoid.
There is the extreme 'supernatural' view which makes far too
sharp a distinction between God the creator and his creation.
Then there is the scientific view at the other extreme which
either denies the existence of God altogether or handcuffs
him to his creation and denies to him his right to intervene in
it. As Hans Küng points out,

the key to the understanding of the New Testament miracle
accounts is not the breach of the laws of nature (which
cannot be verified historically) and not God's universal
government of the world (which is not to be questioned)
but Jesus himself. It is only in the light of his word that his
charismatic deeds acquire their unequivocal meaning.[18]

In other words God does not require of us faith in miracles. It
is not an article of the Creed. But the statement, 'modern man

cannot believe in miracles any more' should be seriously challenged. Actually modern man is ready to believe almost anything. Yet the point I want to make is that man has never been required to build his faith initially on miracles. We are required to believe in Jesus Christ, and the miracles can follow naturally from that basis of faith. In one sense we can leave miracles on one side. After all, Jesus himself said 'Blessed are those who have not seen and yet believe' (Jn 20:29).

The word 'miracle' is notoriously ambiguous and has engaged the sharp minds and pens of many famous theologians, philosophers and scholars. These men have raised issues which people in Jesus' day, including the writers of the gospels, were unaware of. Our problems are not their problems. They were not interested in 'laws of nature' – nor did they follow the rational and scientific approach that we are so familiar with. Miracles were just natural occurrences and it never crossed their minds that any laws were being breached. Miracles were taken for granted.

Now perhaps one can appreciate why I am reticent about attempting to define 'miracles'. Whenever we use the word we do not need to think in terms of the suspension of the laws of nature. We need to see God the creator very much closer to his creation and very much more involved in it than some so-called 'supernaturalists' would allow. We may then be surprised *when* it happens, but not *that* it happens. We shall not need to describe God as 'a miracle-working God'; *for what he does is a natural and normal accompaniment of who he is.*

We should in our examination of the healings of Jesus see that they point continuously to him, not to the healings themselves. It is in our discovery of Jesus that we can best understand his activity. In one sense we can say that, far from breaking the laws of nature, the miracles of Jesus were a restoration to normality of what had deviated from the divine purposes for man. It is death not resurrection which is 'unnatural'. It is illness and demonic possession which break the laws of nature, not the healings of Jesus. We see in the life and ministry of Jesus a return to normality; Jesus is bringing the creation back to its obedience to the Creator. So it is not miracles which are unusual, but their alleged absence in the church and in the world today. In one sense the healings of Jesus are the acted parables of the kingdom, for there was no distinction then between the words and the works of Jesus. The parables were not just pretty stories. They had an inner meaning. They revealed how the world operates. In the miracles we see the other side of the coin. We see the kingdom in operation. The signs and wonders demonstrate the principles of the kingdom. They are the way in which the Lord Jesus Christ was literally 'restoring the kingdom to Israel' (Acts 1:6).

The important matter for us is that Jesus healed people not that he performed miracles. And this ministry of his was a natural and free expression of his relationship to the Father. The miracles have posed a problem for generations of theologians. But a much greater problem would have been the absence of them. It is quite impossible to think of Jesus as the Son of God and not to see his rule over nature in the form of the healings he performed. They were not 'supernatural' happenings, but perfectly natural events in which we see the creation as a mirror of the Creator. As such they have eternal significance and are a constant challenge to us.

Chapter
10

Health and Healing

> Jesus was typically Hebrew in his view of man: he did not
> divide man into body and soul, but he saw him as a whole
> person.
>
> Francis MacNutt

A book about healing has to deal with the theme of health
also. However, the words 'healing' and 'health' meant something very different in biblical times. We need, therefore, to
look at the Old as well as the New Testament. We shall find
that the Old Testament has more to teach us about health
than healing, the New Testament teaches more about healing
than health. Jesus' own understanding of this subject would
have been strongly influenced by the Hebrew understanding
of humanity. His view of life was shaped by his study and
knowledge of the Old Testament. There is strong evidence for
this in the gospels. We must be careful not to read back into
the scriptures our own world view. When Jesus healed the
sick he did it in accordance with a Jewish understanding of
man. Health for him was not, as we so often see it today, the
mere absence of pain or sickness. The Old Testament view of
health was more profound than that.

Health in the Old Testament

It is difficult to find in the Old Testament an exact equivalent
for our word 'health', for the methodology of the Old Testament is different from ours. We seek to arrive at truth by
logical arguments and by careful definition. The Old Testa-

ment method is largely through illustration and example. So it is in the life and character of men and women in the Old Testament that we see the meaning of health. No attempt is made to define what health is.

Another problem arises because the same is true of the word 'body'. There simply is no Old Testament background into which this word can be slotted. The Hebrews had no term for it. In the Septuagint the Greek word *soma* translates eleven Hebrew words and none of them is a true equivalent. There are names for around eighty parts of the body but not one for what we call the 'body' today. The only Hebrew word which has a purely physical meaning is *g viyyah* and it occurs only thirteen times. The Old Testament writers did not require a word for 'body', in a physical sense, because they never regarded the physical body as having reality on its own. The nearest Hebrew word is *basar*, which refers to the physical substance of man, but even here it usually means man in his bodily aspect.

John Robinson in his famous study *The Body* has shown how the Hebrew idea of 'body' is substantially different from the Greek.[1] The western mind, too, is often at variance with the Hebrew. The Old Testament writers make no differentiation between form and matter. *Basar*, therefore, stands for the whole life-substance of man. Even more far-reaching is the fact that the Hebrews opposed the Greek antithesis between body and soul.

The Greek idea of man has been described as 'an angel in a slot machine'. The body was non-essential to the personality. But for the Hebrews the body was essential. Their idea of the personality was an animated body, not an incarnated soul. In other words man does not have a body, he *is* a body.

The significance for us is that the Old Testament writers do not present health primarily in physical terms, because they did not conceive of anything merely in those terms. In this respect their thinking was in marked contrast with the modern popular concept of health, which is mainly seen in physical terms. Jesus, did not, therefore, see his healing role as principally physical. We are inclined to read this back into the

New Testament documents, and in doing so distort the purposes and methods by which Jesus healed the sick in his day. The Old Testament does not divide man into different parts – 'body', 'soul' and 'spirit'. The Hebrews always treated man as a whole and saw health in terms of the whole not the individual parts. They did see aspects of man; but such a view was never allowed to detract from man's essential unity. Also health in the Old Testament could not be divorced from righteousness. It had an ethical context from which it could not be separated. It is not without significance that some modern trends in medicine, are also moving in this direction. Disease is being seen in a wider context, and the growth of what has become known as 'alternative medicine' is a pointer in that direction.

Peace

Some years ago I found myself, when praying for sick people, increasingly using the word 'peace'. I would actually speak 'peace' to diseased tissue and infections. I nearly always used the Hebrew word *shalom*. More recently I have discovered that this is the closest word in the Old Testament for 'health'. It means more than the absence of war, stress, and tension. It declares a state of wholeness. The Hebrews were not concerned with anatomy or physiology. Their interest was in life. They believed that *shalom* was the best word to use to describe a man in a state of wholeness, of being what the Creator had always intended. That is how the Old Testament understood 'health' and it is a million miles from the Roman idea. It is much more all-embracing and always has the overtones of 'righteousness' as an essential part of the peace package.

The word *shalom* comes about 250 times in the Old Testament; about a third of these references come in the Psalms, Isaiah and Jeremiah. Its meaning has been variously given as 'completeness, soundness, welfare'[2] 'soundness, prosperity, well-being'[3] and refers to every area of life – natural as well as personal, mental as well as physical, corporate as well as individual. The final coming of Christ is seen as a reign of peace and one of the messianic titles is 'Prince of Peace'. Peace is only possible in relationship to God, and so the streams of health come from divine not human springs.

The link here with the ministry of Jesus is an interesting one. In an important passage Jesus commissioned the twelve to preach about the kingdom and to 'heal the sick, raise the dead, cleanse lepers, cast out demons' (Mt 10:8). They were told by Jesus that the effect of this ministry would be peace coming to the houses where they were accepted (Mt 10:13). Also we notice that the angelic messengers at the birth of Christ described the occasion as one where there was 'Glory to God . . . and on earth peace among men with whom he is pleased' (Lk 2:14). Peter in one of his talks recorded in Acts spoke of the ministry of Jesus as 'preaching good news of peace' (Acts 10:36).

We need to stress again the relationship between health and righteousness in the understanding of the writers of the Old Testament. It is interesting to notice that the World Health Organization has defined health not only in terms of freedom from disease but also as 'a state of complete physical, mental and social well-being'. The Old Testament takes this a stage further when it relates health to obedience to God's word and law. This can be seen in Exodus 15:26, Leviticus 26:14–16 and Proverbs 3:7–8. Actually Proverbs has numerous references to health and healing which relate closely to its main theme. Thus the wise man will be healthy and free from disease, while the fool 'will be broken beyond healing' (6:15). John Wilkinson has summarised this: 'health (in the Old Testament) is the wholeness of man's being and personality, and the holiness of his character and actions expressed in righteousness and obedience to God's law'.[4]

The Jewish mind was not taken up at all with the questions which are posed by modern psychology and physiology. They were not interested. It is insufficient to say that they were ignorant, although of course they knew little of the facts upon which medical science has been developed. Their major concern was with life itself. This is echoed in the words of Jesus 'what can a man give in return for his life?' Man's relationship to God was what mattered most, not the physiology of how one organ relates to another. And it is this way of thinking which we see in the healing ministry of Jesus. His concern was for righteousness in the whole man, not the temporary amelioration of physical or mental symptoms. He was not interested in healings and miracles for their own sake. His work shows that healing was part of what he came to do, part of the human need which he came not merely to alleviate but to liberate us from.

Health in the New Testament

The New Testament is more concerned with healing than with health, which it more or less presumes. We should not be surprised. Supremely the New Testament is about redemption or deliverance. It tells the story of how God sent his own Son on a mission of restoration, to make good the damage done since man's fall from grace and his departure from innocence. If the teaching about health is assumed in the New Testament, then we can be sure it is the Old Testament understanding of it which is the substance of that assumption.

The Hebrew concept of man is dominated by the theme of 'life'. We see this expressed vividly in the words of Jesus, 'I came that they may have life, and have it abundantly' (Jn 10:10). Abundant life, life lived to the full, is the declared purpose for Christ's coming. There is a new quality of life which is now given to men and women through the life and death of Jesus Christ. It speaks eloquently of a new health factor which brings man through Christ back to the purpose for which he was created, restoring him to the image of God marred since the fall. It is not life on a conveyor belt – human mass production. It has myriads of features, each of which sparkles with its own iridescence. The health which Christ brings is never dull or stereotyped.

The New Testament words which spell out the divine

dimensions of health include the theme of life which we have just dealt with, blessedness, holiness and maturity. Here again we see the consistency of the New Testament testimony as well as its congruity with the Old Testament concept of health. It is all-embracing. It is never narrowly confined to the physical body. The implications are that, if man possesses the life which is 'eternal', everything else will slot into place in its own time.

Another important aspect of this is the way the New Testament uses the verb 'to save' (*sozo*) to describe various healings, including the blind seeing (Mk 10:52), healing from leprosy (Lk 17:19), an issue of blood (Mk 5:34). In each case Jesus said to the sufferer, 'your faith has *saved* you'. The same was also said to a crowd of people who were suffering from unspecified diseases. As many as touched Christ's garment were 'made well' or 'saved' (Mt 14:36).

We are noticing throughout this book how differently the New Testament writers used the Greek language compared with other Greek writers. It is one interesting way by which Christians of the first century sought to show how the Christian view of man is different from that of their pagan neighbours. This comes out in the word 'blessed' (*makarios*). The classical Greek word was *eudaimonia* which means to have a good demon! Since Christians didn't believe there were any good demons, they chose a distinctly inferior word *makarios*.

In the beatitudes in Matthew 5:1–12 Jesus declares the principles of the kingdom of heaven from which health is actually derived. Conversely, when these principles are either ignored or denied, man becomes sick. Here is a complete reversal of so-called normal human values. Ethics are seen as principles of the heart not as convenient pegs on which to hang our behavioural patterns, and which can be moved around to suit the whims and fancies of the age we live in.

We are also called to holiness which is part of wholeness. Paul brings this out clearly in 1 Thessalonians 5:23 when he prays 'May the God of peace himself sanctify you wholly; and may your spirit and soul and body be kept sound and blameless at the coming of our Lord Jesus Christ.' It is interesting to

note again that it is to the God of *peace* that Paul prays. The
NEB translates this verse – 'May God . . . make you holy in
every part, and keep you sound . . .' The prayer covers the
whole of man – spirit, soul and body – the complicated
interaction of many parts and aspects of our humanity. Paul is
not dissecting man into three distinct parts as the Greek
philosophers did with their own brand of precision. Rather in
using the words 'sanctify you wholly' he is emphasising not the
distinctiveness of the parts, but the unity of the whole. Here in
this verse are contained the four qualities of the divine which
were first imparted to man at creation and which are now
re-imparted by divine grace – peace, holiness, soundness and
blamelessness.

Making men whole

The healings of Jesus seem a far cry from the triumphant
advance of medical science during this century. We should be
grateful to God for much of this progress, leading as it has to
better health and the alleviation of pain. But there have been
several medical hiccups in recent years. There is a growing
reaction within the medical profession to some areas of
orthodox medicine, not least its dependence on drugs, which
in the long term can fail to provide the cures they were meant
to. Today there is a growing acceptance of alternative
methods, hence the new name – alternative medicine.
Homeopathy pioneered the new approach, which has all
along received little recognition from the medical profession.

A major breakthrough came in 1973 when three eminent
American doctors gave a favourable report on acupuncture
following a fact-finding visit to China. Only a few years earlier
a leading American pharmacologist, Louis Lasagne, had
derisively dismissed it as 'superstition and ignorance'. I am
not qualified to comment on acupuncture itself, but I'm
simply using it as an illustration of a change in emphasis, for
its importance is that it has brought into question the principles of physiology upon which much of medicine has for

centuries been based. Acupuncture is practised on the basis of unseen 'canals' which are charted – and which are claimed to be real, though not material. The novelty of such a proposition would, if accepted, undermine the excessively 'physical' understanding of the human frame and open doors into 'spiritual' dimensions which have in the past been almost totally ignored. Did the healing ministry of Jesus operate in this kind of area simply because the Jewish mind had never understood our humanity any other way? If so, conventional physiology would be found lacking a vital dimension – and so would psychology.

It has long been accepted that imagination can exercise an important part in the healing process. But alternative medicine has gone further than that. It has served notice that it is challenging the very dogmas which the high priests of the medical world have preached for many generations. A man called F. G. Crookshank summarised this assault on medical sacred cows over fifty years ago by saying, 'organic disease is what we say we cure, but don't; functional disease is what quacks cure, and we wish we could'. But the majority of today's disorders are functional anyway, so that should open the doors for new dimensions to balance the overemphasis of the past. There are signs too that the general public is far from satisfied with the way medical science has been going in recent years, and many are turning to what has also been called 'fringe medicine'.

The British consumer magazine *Which?* conducted a survey in 1983 which revealed that ninety per cent were satisfied with the 'fringe' treatment they had received. Other reports indicate less confidence in straightforward and traditional medical treatment. Ehrlich's dream in the 1950s of 'magic bullets', drugs capable of curing every known disease, has proved a false hope. The turnover of new drugs is frightening; many seem only to relieve symptoms, reduce pain, but they can often produce harmful side effects, which in some cases have proved fatal. Ruth West and Brian Inglis in an article in *The Times*[5] reported on clofigrate, marketed in the 1960s, which did lower blood cholesterol and so protect patients from heart attacks. This was proved to be effective in rats, but it was discovered that the mortality rate from all causes was twenty-five percent higher amongst those taking this drug than those who hadn't.

The Prince of Wales caused a stir when addressing the British Medical Association in 1983 by referring to 'those ancient and unconscious forces so vital to our unity with nature'. Prince Charles was touching something vital when he referred to 'our unity with nature'. The Hebrew understanding of humanity is much closer to this wider and 'holistic' viewpoint than the narrower view which is almost universally accepted by the medical profession and is still the ruling principle. It was this understanding, when applied to human sickness on the grand scale, which made Jesus' approach so effective and revolutionary. We are told by John that Jesus 'knew mankind to the core' (Jn 2:24 Living Bible).

We need, however, to be aware of the dangers. Jesus was not alone in the field of 'faith healing'. Magic was practised universally in the Roman empire, and charlatans were two-a-penny. The hesitation which the BMA and other like-minded professional bodies have towards fringe medicine is understandable. Some of it is subject to deception and chicanery. The public does need to be protected. The setting up of the British Holistic Medical Association is a step in this direction. The 'ancient and unconscious forces' to which the Prince of Wales referred in his speech are not always benign; some can be distinctly malevolent, and much of Jesus' ministry, as we shall see, was directed towards delivering people from such forces. One is moving into territory which can be dangerous, where opposing spiritual forces battle for the bodies and souls of men.

Jesus' mission

Jesus' task was to make men whole in order that society might be healed. To do this they had to be set free. The basis upon which Jesus healed the sick was his own understanding of his mission. It was the kingdom he came to inaugurate, one which was to be different from every kind of earthly structure or community. He saw men and women deprived of the ability to respond to their high calling to be children of God and children of that kingdom. He saw their minds disturbed, and their bodies diseased. Man was created in the image of God so that he might instinctively, by virtue of his created being, respond to God, and walk with him in innocence and peace. Man was created to be part of the divine community, to have communion and fellowship with God. Adam and Eve in the Garden had no need to hide themselves from God or from each other.

But then it all began to go wrong. Adam and Eve listened to another voice contradicting God's. They fell for the temptation to become independent of God. The result was immediate, they had to hide from God. Paradise was lost. Mankind was cursed. Man became alienated from God, alienated from nature (in that they were embarrassed by their nakedness) and alienated from each other: 'From now on you and the woman will be enemies, as will all of your offspring and heirs' (Gen 3:15, Living Bible). The very soil was cursed. Man became an alien within his own environment. The ground was no longer man's friend. Instead he had to subdue it by the sweat of his brow. Battle commenced.

The fall, the effects of which Jesus Christ came to deliver mankind from, has been variously interpreted. But there are several features of it which cast light on the healings of Jesus. The first one I want to refer to is loss of contact.

Loss of contact

God is revealed in the Old Testament as the Creator in constant contact with his creation. Although in one sense outside it (Christians are not pantheists) he is constantly at work in it, and the writers attribute much of the workings of nature to his handiwork. The sun, stars, moon and planets are not only made by him, but they work for him and it is God who determines and sustains their existence. As Paul puts it in Colossians 'it is his power that holds everything together' (1:17, Living Bible). The same is also true of the crown of his creation – man himself. There is what theologians have chosen to call 'a general providence' which describes God's ultimate authority and power over mankind, in which in a general sense he guides and directs our individual destinies. By nature man is a rebel. But God has his own way of tapping even man's rebelliousness and turning it to good. However, the fall seriously impaired man's point of contact with God. In fact the natural instinct implanted by God in man for fellowship with him was so interfered with that Adam and Eve tried to hide from God (as if that were ever possible!).

The supreme mission of Jesus was to heal this gravely disturbed relationship and restore men and women to their real vocation which is close fellowship with God. One aspect of this is the interesting emphasis in the New Testament on healings which relate to man's senses. The blind received their sight, the deaf were able to hear, the mutes talked and the stutterers spoke plainly. Those who were previously unable to communicate with their families and friends now found they could. And what a sensation this was to them! The first face the blind saw was always Jesus'; the first words the deaf heard were from his lips and the first words the dumb spoke were addressed in praise to Jesus. They were in contact again.

These healings were parables as well as miracles, for they pointed, as all the miracles of Jesus do, to the ultimate purposes for which the Son of God ministered to people – to bring them to God. Jesus' interest was not only that the handicapped could overcome their disabilities, and be physically able to relate on an equality with their fellow human beings. That was good and important in itself. But what was infinitely more important was that blind men could see God, the deaf hear him and the dumb sing his praises. It was contact with God that was chiefly at stake and the purpose of Christ's long-expected coming was to re-establish in his kingdom the close fellowship for which man was created and without which he cannot be whole.

Disintegration

Disintegration was the baleful result of man's alienation from God, the first bitter fruits of which were harvested at the fall. Man became a split personality. He not only lost contact with the reality of God, he ceased to be a real person in his own right. The relationship between the man and the woman degenerated quickly. They were soon blaming each other for what had happened. A civil war broke out within the created universe which divided what God had united.

The purpose for which the Son of God came and died was to reintegrate and reunite what man by his disobedience had caused to be confused and divided. Paul writes that the plan of God is 'to unite all things in him, things in heaven and things on earth' (Eph 1:10). It is man who has separated his body from the whole spiritual dimension that distinguishes man from the lower forms of creation. For only man was created in the image of God. Thus we think we can handle the physical aspect of our nature as if the other parts did not exist, or on the other hand deal with the spiritual dimension as if the body wasn't part of it. We need to see that we cannot escape from either the spiritual or the physical. Man cannot be wholly saved by drugs or medical treatment, nor can he detach his body from his spiritual life. The very biblical language and understanding of man makes it obligatory for us to have a healing ministry which relates the spiritual to the physical and the physical to the spiritual. By ignoring the one we do a disservice to the other and are ignoring human and divine realities.

There was something distinctly macabre about Lord Rutherford bicycling through the streets of Cambridge telling people 'we've split the atom'. It was not long before the sinister mushroom-clouds over Hiroshima and Nagasaki were for some the signs of man's doom and ultimate self-destruction. 'Nothing that they propose to do will now be impossible for them' said the Lord while he viewed the rising tower of Babel. Whether it was right or wrong for nuclear research to be taken into the dangerous territory of armaments has been endlessly debated. Perhaps this step is the ultimate one of man's regression in the process of disintegration. But we see it even more vividly in the field of politics and economics. Man seems to be irreversibly committed to the atomising process whereby he is split apart and separated from all that previously held him together. The wholesale breakdown of family life, the rising tide of divorce, the division of the world into permanently estranged camps. The haves and the have-nots. Catholics and Protestants in Northern Ireland, Arabs and Jews in the Middle East, Indians and Spaniards in Latin America are a few examples. And because man cannot divorce all this from the physical realities of life, he has had to pay a heavy price in the form of sickness and disease. Cancer has been described as 'exuberant growth without order'. It is cells in rebellion against the Creator. They are doing their own thing, a course of action which in the end can prove fatal.

Jesus Christ came to reintegrate man, to bring new harmony and peace to man – body, soul and spirit. His healings were vivid illustrations of this. He literally liberated people from sickness. He took Isaiah 61 on his lips – 'He has sent me to . . . set at liberty those who are oppressed' (Lk 4:18). Thus a woman 'bound by Satan' is released so that her back literally straightened up when before it had been bent (Lk 13:10–17). He saw men and women who were the victims of their own or other people's sin and weakness. He came to put together what man had divided. We see this particularly in healings from neurological diseases. When man's nervous system is tampered with it can cause paralysis, or impaired organ functions. Epilepsy is another result of the malfunctioning of the nervous system. When this happens the body is unable to function properly. Limbs and organs cannot obey directions from the head. Man, as a result, is unable to be what he was always intended to be.

The primacy of health

It is easy for us in concentrating on the healings of Jesus to lose sight of and even forget altogether the primary concern of God which is the healthiness of his people. We know today, as never so fully before, that the healthiness of the body cannot be detached from the rest of human life, our personalities, the formation of our characters, the development of our sexuality, and the instruction of our minds. Jesus knew this and ministered most of the time at several levels at once. It was not just a matter of clearing away symptoms. Man's wholeness, health at every level, was the Lord's ultimate goal, and he always steered his patients in that direction, taking them as far as they were prepared to go with him. All he asked for was cooperation, which he sometimes received and sometimes didn't.

Chapter 11

The Gospel of the Kingdom

> Indeed I have seen the kingdom of God come with power.
>
> George Whitefield, June 1739

George Whitefield described a huge meeting on Kennington Common in South London as the coming of the kingdom 'with power'. In the eighteenth century the Evangelical Revival was seen by its leaders as the fruit of preaching the gospel of the kingdom. People were being brought to their knees. They were acknowledging Jesus Christ as Lord. The meetings themselves could not be merely rationally explained; other forces were at work, which they attributed to the power of the Holy Spirit, who was 'bringing in the Kingdom'. For over 200 years Evangelicals have consistently seen the kingdom mainly in this context. For them the biblical theme of the kingdom of God is another word for evangelism.

Looking through the New Testament one must agree that this is a fair assessment, although it certainly does not exhaust the meaning of the word 'kingdom'. During the nineteenth century a new interpretation emerged, in which the kingdom of God was seen in terms of social and economic justice, God's concern for the poor, underprivileged, blacks, prisoners of conscience, and other victims of oppression. The gospel of the kingdom began to be seen in terms of liberating such people. Later in the twentieth century the World Council of Churches was to become the chief rallying point for such concerns. It has become the champion of those fighting racism, sexism, and every other form of social and economic injustice.

The first and second views of the kingdom are often in conflict. This came sharply into focus at the Uppsala Assembly of the WCC, especially in the Report *The Church for Others*, which gave currency to a new vocabulary of mission. In this report God is seen to be at work in the historical process and the purpose of his mission is to establish social harmony or *shalom*. *Shalom* seems to be identical with the kingdom of God. At Uppsala the social change envisaged by the use of the word 'kingdom' left little or no room for evangelistic concern. At a plenary session of the Assembly John Stott protested about this. He said that he agreed with the concern the Assembly had expressed for the hunger, poverty and injustices in the world, 'but I do not find a comparable concern or compassion for the spiritual hunger of men', he said. 'The church's first priority remains the millions who being without Christ are perishing.' I recommend John Stott's book *Christian Mission in the Modern World*, from which these words are taken, for its clarity in dealing with the tension points which exist between these two interpretations of the kingdom.[1]

But there is a third view, which does not necessarily conflict with the other two, and which is significantly different. In many ways it is nearer to the biblical texts than the other two, and is the most relevant to our subject.

Jesus' key-note teaching

If one was asked to sum up the teaching of Jesus in one word it would surely be 'kingdom'. It is the central theme of his message and runs like a golden thread from beginning to end.

It was John the Baptist, Jesus' forerunner, who first used the phrase in the New Testament (see Mt 3:2). We find Jesus also using it at the start of his ministry. 'From that time Jesus began to preach, saying, "Repent, for the kingdom of heaven is at hand"' (Mt 4:17). From then onwards the word 'kingdom' is often on the lips of Jesus. There is no agreement as to how far John the Baptist and Jesus were taking over a slogan which had arisen in the context of Jewish expectations of the future. The central focus of this was to be the decisive intervention of God to restore Israel to its former independence and Davidic glories. But, though Jesus' understanding of the nature and character of the kingdom differed from this popular approach, by using the word 'kingdom' he was certainly keying into expectations which were central to the aspirations of his contemporaries. It was what they wanted to hear, even if their vision for the future needed refocusing. Jesus, in other words, was right on their wavelength.

It soon becomes clear that Jesus' teaching about the kingdom had a present and a future aspect. It truly was 'at hand', meaning within reach of everyone. Yet it was also 'still to come', so much so that the disciples, when taught by Jesus how to pray, were told to say 'thy kingdom come . . .' There is an inevitable tension between the two aspects. We live in what some have called the 'overlap' between the kingdom which is already here and the one that is yet to come. Actually it is the same kingdom – only with two aspects, one present and one future.

The kingdom here and now

The references to this aspect of the kingdom are not numerous. However, it was the dominant reality of Jesus' ministry. When he cast out evil spirits he declared 'the kingdom of God has come upon you' (Mt 12:28). It is in this area of his ministry that the present reality of the kingdom is so palpably visible. When John the Baptist was having doubts while in prison whether his cousin Jesus was really the Messiah, thinking perhaps that he and his disciples ought to be looking for another, the one sent to enquire of Jesus returned with a catalogue of signs and wonders. 'Go and tell John what you have seen and heard' Jesus said, 'the blind receive their sight, the lame walk, lepers are cleansed, and the deaf hear, the dead are raised up, the poor have good news preached to them' (Lk 7:22).

So we see that healing from sickness and deliverance from Satan, are both offered as present realities. The kingdom of God can be both 'seen' and 'entered' here and now, and a prominent Jewish Rabbi was rebuked for not knowing this (John 3:1–15). Jesus, in the years of his earthly ministry, was the king reigning in his kingdom here on earth, taking authority over sickness and Satan, and claiming authority to forgive sins. The gospels are full of personal declarations of absolute authority. There can be no kingdom without a king. In Jesus his contemporaries saw and heard kingly rule and power exercised.

The future kingdom

We cannot do justice to the concept of the kingdom if we do not include the future aspect alongside the present. The kingdom of God is likened by Jesus in some of his parables to seed growing in the ground. There is a present reality, which is often hidden and secret; but there is to be a harvest in the future when the full purposes of the kingdom will be revealed openly. It is only when the corn of wheat falls into the ground and dies that the future harvest is assured (Jn 12:24). The fullest manifestations of the kingdom will be in the future. The Jewish expectation, which limited the boundaries of the kingdom to Israel, was too narrow. The question asked by the disciples after Jesus' resurrection reflect that viewpoint, 'Lord, will you at this time restore the kingdom to *Israel*?' (Acts 1:6). But Jesus wanted them to have a much wider and deeper understanding and expectation. They were to be Spirit-filled witnesses, not only in Jerusalem, but 'to the end of the earth' (Acts 1:8). In that sense the kingdom is still future. Nevertheless it is firmly and irrevocably anchored in space and time. The kingdom, whatever its future manifestations may be, is here and now present amongst the people of God.

The kingdom and healings of Jesus

It is quite impossible to think about 'the healings of Jesus' without considering his teaching about the kingdom of God. For Jesus teaching and action flowed together. 'Healing must be interpreted in the light of the kingdom of God', John Wimber insists.[2] Jesus' teaching brought healing and his healings were lessons in themselves. They were acted parables. To sharply divide the one from the other is to distort both. To understand the healings we need to understand Jesus' teaching about the kingdom; conversely, to grasp the full meaning of the kingdom we need to keep in mind the healings and deliverances which were a marked feature of Jesus' life and ministry.

The phrase 'the gospel of the kingdom' comes three times in Matthew's gospel. In two cases it describes the ministry of Jesus and the wording is almost identical. 'He went about all Galilee, teaching in their synagogues and preaching the gospel of the kingdom and healing every disease and every infirmity among the people' (Mt 4:23). In Matthew 9:35 the locality is different, but the wording the same. Obviously we are meant to see an important link between 'the gospel of the kingdom' and his actual ministry of healing and deliverance. It could be argued that we cannot make an exact identification, and say that the gospel of the kingdom *is* healing and deliverance. But there is no way of denying that the two are closely linked to each other, so that we can say that the one leads inevitably to the other.

In Matthew 12:14–32 there is, however, an exact identification between the two. All successful people have enemies and Jesus was no exception. The more successful he was the more enemies there were. The more he healed people, the more his opponents had to find other explanations. The evidence was there for all to see, so the only way they could explain it away was to blame it on Satan. Jesus retorted that if Satan casts out Satan, 'he is divided against himself' (v. 26). He went on to say, 'if it is by the Spirit of God that I cast out demons, *then the kingdom of God has come upon you*'

(v. 28). The casting out of demons *is* the coming of the kingdom.

Jesus' kingdom programme

The third instance of the phrase 'the gospel of the kingdom' in Matthew's gospel is a missionary imperative declaring Jesus' programme on earth until his return at the end of the age, 'and this gospel of the kingdom will be preached throughout the whole world, as a testimony to all nations; and then the end will come' (Mt 24:14). By specifying it as 'this gospel' Jesus is declaring that it is the same gospel which he had been preaching for the past three years. Since both the other verses directly link the healing of disease with the gospel of the kingdom, the preaching of the gospel of the kingdom should normally include the ministry of healing.

There is a further indication of this when we examine Jesus' commissioning of the twelve and the seventy for their ministry. This should not surprise us, for Jesus said, 'A disciple is not above his teacher, nor a servant above his master; it is enough for the disciple to be like his teacher, and the servant like his master' (Mt 10:24–25). These words were spoken to the disciples just before they were sent out. We would, therefore, expect the disciples to model their ministry on his. In John's gospel, Jesus encouraged his people to do just that, 'he who believes in me will also do the works that I do' (Jn 14:12). So the twelve are told to preach as Jesus had that 'the kingdom of heaven is at hand', but also to 'heal the sick, raise the dead, cleanse lepers, cast out demons' (Mt 10:7–8).

Luke's account is even more specific, 'and he sent them out to preach the kingdom of God and to heal' (Lk 9:2). When the seventy are sent out, they are told 'heal the sick . . . and say to them, "The kingdom of God has come near to you"' (Lk 10:9). We thus see in all these references the close identification between the kingdom of God and the healing ministry. When people are healed the kingdom has come, and to preach the kingdom, means amongst other things, healing the

sick and delivering the demonised. Whatever other interpretations of the kingdom we may put forward, this is one
which is clear in the New Testament. And the preaching of
this gospel of the kingdom is mandatory on the church until
the return of Christ, according to Matthew 24:14. It is to be
proclaimed throughout the world and only when this has been
done will Christ return.

Final instructions

The importance of the gospel of the kingdom comes out even
more strongly when we look at the final instructions given to
the church's leaders by Jesus after his resurrection.

1. Matthew (Mt 28:18–20)

Jesus makes it clear that he is the one with supreme authority
'in heaven and on earth' (v. 18). He has the right to say 'Go
therefore and make disciples' (v. 19), and we have the responsibility to obey him. Jesus told them to teach new disciples 'to observe all that I have commanded you' (v. 20).
Since Jesus had commanded them to heal the sick and set
people free from evil spirits, we must assume that was to be
part of the teaching they were to pass on to all future
generations of Christians, and that these Christians were to
'observe' or do such works. There had been no separation in
Jesus' ministry between teaching and doing. *He taught and
did the kingdom. So must we.*

2. Mark (Mk 16:9–20)

As in the rest of the book I do not propose to deal with the
textual problems of the so-called 'longer ending' of Mark's
gospel. In my opinion the authorship is not important. Every
word of the passage is consistent with the Acts of the
Apostles, and so can be accepted whoever the author was.

The command of Jesus is again clear, 'go into all the world
and preach the gospel to the whole creation . . . these signs

will accompany those who believe: in my name they will cast out demons; they will speak in new tongues; they will pick up serpents, and if they drink any deadly thing, it will not hurt them; they will lay hands on the sick, and they will recover' (vv. 15, 17–18).

Jesus expected his followers to continue his successful ministry of signs and wonders. Although the word 'kingdom' is not mentioned, it is kingdom-type ministry which is in view, one like that of Jesus himself who came 'preaching the gospel of God, and saying, "the time is fulfilled, and the kingdom of God is at hand; repent, and believe in the gospel"' (Mk 1:14–15).

3. Luke (Lk 24:44–49; Acts 1:6–8)

Luke is the chief witness to Pentecost. Although not present himself, he describes it in considerable detail. What is important for us to see is that he closely links the promise of the power of the Holy Spirit with the future ministry of the church, and shows in Acts that the early church understood it in terms of power evangelism, a ministry of signs and wonders in demonstration that the kingdom of God had come. Thus the final instructions of Jesus are closely related to their need to wait for the anointing power of the Spirit, so they might go out in that power to bring the gospel of the kingdom to the nations.

4. John (Jn 20:21–23)

John of all the authors of the gospels insists that the signs were the key to Jesus' successful ministry. They form the main framework of this gospel, written so clearly to win the hearts of unbelievers. It is John alone who recalls for us the raising of Lazarus from the dead four days after he had passed away.

Thus when Jesus says to the church leaders, 'As the Father has sent me, even so I send you' (v. 21) he is affirming that his ministry, which includes healing and deliverance, is going to continue through them. We again see that Jesus' final instructions regarding the future of the church contain the ministry of healing.

A Third Force

Since the turn of the century there has been a widespread new movement in the churches which in the 1950s and early 1960s earned the respect of theologians like Bishop Lesslie Newbigin, Professor John Mackay and Dr Pitt Van Dusen. Lesslie Newbigin included this new stream alongside the Catholic and Protestant in his famous book *The Household of God*.[3] Pitt Van Dusen in an article in *Life* called it 'the Third Force in Christendom'. This movement has various streams of its own, of which three predominate. The first is the independent stream which brought into being the Pentecostal churches at the beginning of the twentieth century and in the last few years has given rise to other kinds of independent churches. The second is the charismatic stream, usually called charismatic because it describes a similar movement to the Pentecostal, but distinguished from it because of its place within the historic churches – Roman Catholic, Anglican, Lutheran, Methodist etc. The third stream is that of the Third World independent churches, mostly in Africa and Asia, many of which began prior to decolonisation, but which have mushroomed in the new emerging nations since they received their independence. If all these were added together they would (in 1980) probably number in excess of 115 million Christians.[4]

This great world movement arose in different ways in different countries and churches. But the common thread which runs through them all is the conviction that the gifts of the Holy Spirit are available today and, if the Holy Spirit is invoked, they will be given to all God's people. Such a movement sees the signs and wonders as part of that 'gospel of the kingdom' which Jesus said must be preached to all nations before he returns. Thus the kingdom or the rule of God is extended to include the power and authority of God over satanic powers (deliverance ministry or exorcism) and over sickness and disease. The movement now has some of the fastest growing churches in the world.

A healing kingdom

It is important to understand the relationship between the kingdom of God and the healings of Jesus. Both spoke loudly and clearly to Jesus' contemporaries. Sickness, disease, and the invasion of the human mind and personality by false ideologies and satanic influences, are all ways by which the world is diverted from the divine purposes for which it was created. The way back is to respond to the kingdom so that God's will is done 'on earth as it is in heaven'. Therefore, when Jesus healed the sick and cast out evil spirits he was bringing in the kingdom as surely as when he forgave men their sins and urged Nicodemus to be 'born again' and thus to enter the kingdom. The charismatic dimension of the kingdom is explicit in the New Testament and we should face the implications of this today. *It is impossible to do full justice to the doctrine of the kingdom of God if we ignore the charismatic character of it.*

It is unfortunate that the word 'kingdom' for many refers exclusively to the area of the socio-political – the combatting of racism, sexism, restoring human rights and economic justice. The charismatic interpretation, which is clearly a part of the New Testament understanding of the kingdom, is often ignored or even scoffed at as either naive or pietistic.

In his book *Christianity Rediscovered*, Vincent Donovan, a Roman Catholic priest who has worked mostly in the Third World, writes,

> our business as Christians is the establishment of the King-
> dom. It is a kingdom that takes its beginnings here in this
> real world, and aims at the fulfilling of this world, of
> bringing this world to its destiny. But it is not a kingdom
> that can be identified with the Roman Empire any more

than it can be identified with a capitalist paradise or a Marxist utopia. The dimensions of this Kingdom reach to domains that politics can never reach, to the realms of the 'Kingdom that is not of this world'. It is that extra dimension that Christians are called on to participate in making a reality. Politics as well as everything else that is human and earthly has its place in the establishment of this kingdom. But the political reality is not the ultimate reality, nor is it the sole instrument for the bringing of the kingdom.[5]

Jesus preached the gospel of the kingdom on a broader canvas than we do. Shut in as we often are by our own predilections, blind to our narrowness of outlook and unable to detect the tunnel vision we nearly all suffer from, no wonder our understanding of the kingdom is distorted by what we leave out of it. We should allow the Holy Spirit to remove the blinkers we have, so that we can see the full scope of the kingdom.

It is easy to cling tenaciously to what we see of the truth because it has captured our hearts and imaginations. But the dimensions God wants to bring his people into, and the unity that will come as a fruit of it, will never be experienced if we hold back. There are important prizes to be obtained for those with the courage to hold together all that the New Testament tells us about the kingdom.

Chapter 12

Faith, Authority and Inspiration

> Christian thinkers cannot consider experiences of heal-
> ing today because of the tacit acceptance of a world view
> which allows no place for a breakthrough of divine
> power into the space-time world.
>
> Morton Kelsey

The present western world view does, I believe, shut God out
of his universe. If once we allow that God can and will at times
break into the space-time world of ours, then the door opens
wide to healings in the name of Jesus in our day. This is made
doubly important when we recognise the primary place that
healings had in the ministry of Jesus in the first century. If we
are meant to be imitators of him, why not in the healing
ministry? We also need to recognise the high incidence of
sickness throughout the world. The affluent west spends huge
sums of money every year to keep its citizens reasonably
healthy. Very few families are free from some form of chronic
illness or disability, and none are free from sickness
altogether. If we include, as we should, mental illnesses, then
we live in a sick world and we all know that the normal process
of degeneration ultimately leads to death. So it is not surprising, judging from the amount of literature on the subject, that
man has an insatiable interest in his health and well-being,
and will go to all lengths to secure it.

In the light of this we should expect a crowd whenever
someone has a message about a God who heals the sick. It
happened with Jesus and it will happen today. Jesus' cousin
John also drew large crowds to hear a stern message about
repentance. The media knows that bad news sells best.

However, John was not to keep his captive audience. The fickle crowds gave up this eccentric prophet for the new celebrity who not only spoke about the kingdom of God but actually demonstrated its power through signs and wonders.

Whose faith?

It is clear from reading the gospels that faith played an important part in Jesus' healing ministry. We learn more about faith in relationship to the miracles than to anything else. In the synoptic gospels nearly two-thirds of the references to faith occur in relationship to the miracles, and almost all of these occur in the sayings of Jesus, who either encourages or recommends it, or rebukes people for their lack of it. James Dunn commenting on this says that it reflects 'a typical attitude of Jesus'.[1]

Jesus was always on the lookout for faith, rejoicing whenever he saw it, groaning and even weeping when he didn't. Jesus' human frailty is starkly presented to us when we are told that in Nazareth he was unable to do much because of the presence of unbelief. Dunn comments, 'faith in the recipient as it were completed the circuit so that the power could flow'.[2] There was nothing magical about the power that Jesus exercised. He depended for success on winning a response. The power Jesus had at his disposal was not like that of an eastern potentate, to do with it as he wished. Jesus' charismatic power came from God not from the occult world of magic.

Yet in none of these passages is there any mention of the faith of Jesus. In every single case it is the faith of other people who are responding to something they see, hear or feel about Jesus. Jesus never mollycoddled people. They had to respond and often take the initiative themselves. They may not have had much faith, but what they did have they were to make available. This is not to say, of course, that Jesus did not have faith. Rather it is saying the opposite. Jesus was full of faith.

But he used the faith he had to inspire others to faith, not to let his faith take the place of theirs. One translation of Galatians 2:20 is 'the faith of the Son of God'. Paul there claims that Jesus' faith is the source of his own. Jesus did not browbeat people into believing. He drew faith out of them. The fire of faith, however dimly it may have burned, was fanned not quenched by the sensitive words and actions of Jesus. Dunn puts it well, 'Jesus is the witness of grace, not the witness of faith'.[3]

If this is so, then the church should not shrink from its responsibility to be a believing community, but should open the way for the Son of God to heal the sick today as he did in the days of his flesh. There is no lack of will or desire on the part of Jesus. Neither is there any shortage of people needing healing. But he will not normally do it without faith on our part. Jesus reserved his most scathing words for those who did not believe.

Whose authority?

It was not long before Jesus was being challenged as to the authority with which he was healing the sick. It was to continue as a bone of contention between himself and the Jewish authorities to the hour of his death. While walking in the temple during his final week on earth he was asked, 'By what authority are you doing these things?' (Mk 11:28). People noticed the authority that Jesus had and it impressed the Roman centurion so much that he asked Jesus to heal his sick slave with words from a distance (Lk 7:1–10). In the synoptic gospels the astonishment of the crowds was as much a response to the authority (*exousia*) of his ministry as it was to its power (*dunamis*). Jesus' very presence at times inspired awe and humility, so that both the ruler of the synagogue (Mk 5:22), and the demonised (e.g. Mk 3:11 and 5:7), knelt at his feet. Jesus never demanded this of anyone. A person who has real authority never has to. People just accept it. In Mark 10:32 there is a striking reference to Jesus striding ahead of his disciples with such a sense of purpose and destiny that they were 'amazed' or 'filled with awe'. Jesus' presence, even the way he walked, spoke of authority. It is this more than anything else which infuriated his enemies.

On a few occasions Jesus actually claimed this authority in public notably in Mark 2:10 where he spoke of his authority to forgive sins. In Luke 10:19 he gave authority, which he had already demonstrated in his own ministry, to his disciples to crush their satanic foes. But Jesus' authority was different from that of his human adversaries. They had official authority, he had charismatic. James Dunn comments on this authority, 'the one who already in his lifetime provoked such respect and even awe in his presence is one who had divine charisma'.[4] Jesus' was the prototype of all future Spirit-filled ministries. Such people usually provoke hostility for much the same reasons. Their spiritual authority turns them into potential popularists, and sets them against the more stodgy and commonplace authority which comes through human appointment. Jesus had a mysterious ability to inspire fear and awe on the one hand, and yet to draw certain kinds of people, particularly the underprivileged and weak, close to himself. He was a man of the people who held his position only through what he received from God. His authority came from heaven not from man. This was the basis for his brilliant answer to the challenge presented to him by his enemies in Mark 11:28, 'Was the baptism of John from heaven or from men?' (v. 30). His enemies knew that John was another 'unofficial' celebrity, and so they found they could not answer him.

The charisma of Jesus is seen more vividly in his battles with his enemies than in his healing miracles. Everyone who met Jesus had to make a response. He was that sort of person. You either loved him or you hated him. You either followed him or you plotted to do him to death. You either believed him to be the Son of God or an agent of the devil. Neutrality seemed to be impossible in his presence.

Whose inspiration?

Two facts come out clearly in the healing work of Christ. Jesus attributed his power and authority to the Holy Spirit, and the directions he received for his life to the Father. In this respect he was no different in the days of his flesh from anyone else. He told the Pharisees that he cast out Satan by the Holy Spirit (Mt 12:28). Peter in Acts 10:38 declared how God 'anointed Jesus of Nazareth with the Holy Spirit and with power'. He went on to say what were the results of this anointing, 'he went about doing good and healing all that were oppressed by the devil, for God was with him'. Jesus' ability to heal and cast out spirits was derived from his anointing at his baptism by the Holy Spirit. In other words Jesus' authority to do the things he did came more from the third person than the second person of the trinity.

The importance of Jesus' relationship to the Father is even more strikingly revealed in the gospels, and comes out most fully in John's gospel. One of the clearest statements is in Luke 10:21–22. The disciples had just returned triumphantly from their first taste of a deliverance ministry. They had discovered that 'even the demons are subject to us in your name'. We have a brief glimpse of the intimacy of Jesus' prayer relationship with his Father. He rejoiced in the Holy Spirit, and then thanked his Father for revealing the secrets of the kingdom to 'babes'. He went on, 'yea, Father, for such was thy gracious will'. Thus Jesus saw the will of his Father being implemented by the disciples just as it had been in his own ministry. Then he affirmed that he had received everything from his Father (v. 22).

In John's gospel this flash of insight is embellished and enlarged. Jesus acknowledges that what he knows flows out of this experience with the Father (3:10–13, 31b–35), who has given him the Spirit without measure. We remember that at the very moment of anointing the words come from heaven, 'Thou art my beloved Son; with thee I am well pleased' (Lk 3:22). The relationship is even more explicitly stated in John 5:17–21. Jesus says that he works with the Father, and does nothing on his own initiative. He does things and speaks words only on the basis of what he sees and hears from the Father. John Wimber writes, 'Jesus lives on the principle of explicit revelation and implicit obedience'.[5]

This theme is further expanded in John 7:15–18, 46. Jesus' concern is to honour his Father. He is not concerned with his own position or glory. Out of this vital attitude of total trust and obedience there comes real authority in what he says and does. The Father has given everything into his hands (Jn 3:35). In John 8:16, 26–29, 38 we see the relationship between the Father and the Son as one of complete trust and commitment. Jesus is concerned always to be pleasing to the Father. Thus in John 10:30, 37–38 we read that they are 'one'. Jesus speaks of his miracles as 'the works of my Father'.

It is this kind of relationship that the Lord also wants us to develop. When he saw it in his disciples he rejoiced in the Holy Spirit (Lk 10:21). Jesus' inspiration should also be ours, for at Pentecost he gave the church the power of the Holy Spirit, while at Calvary he made possible for us a relationship with the Father like the one he knew during his life on earth. Both the benefits of Calvary, which made possible a relationship of intimacy with the Father through the removal of our sins and our total identification with him, and the power of Pentecost through the anointing of the Holy Spirit are God's gifts to us today. We cannot heal the sick and deliver people from the power of Satan without them. If the Son of God depended on the Father for direction and the Spirit for the dynamic, so surely should we. We too can hear the words of God; we can know his thoughts, and do the works that the Son of God did – and even greater ones – now that the Son has been glorified and has poured out the Spirit on the church.

Ministering healing

Our study has shown that the gospels do not present us with an instruction book on how to heal the sick. If we are to follow the Master Healer, then we need to know the Father who guided him and the Spirit who empowered him. Without direction and power we shall only be playing games with people. We need to be open to the surprises of the Holy Spirit, flexible and humble-minded, ready to learn from our mistakes, and always open to reason. Jesus loved people and was prepared to give himself unreservedly to them. He knew the difference between the strong who needed humbling and the weak who needed encouragement. Yet he also knew the dangers inherent in this kind of work, the neuroses of the crowd, the adulation of personalities, and greed for success and popularity. These he avoided with great care.

We have seen that, although the apostles had a special calling to heal the sick, Jesus never intended it to be restricted to the apostolic band. We have already noted there is precedence for elders having a special calling to heal the sick (James 5:14), and one of the marks of an apostle was miraculous power including signs and wonders (2 Cor 12:12). But equally we need to notice that Jesus' policy from the beginning was increasingly to delegate his authority to his disciples, first to the twelve, then the seventy, and finally to the whole church. He wanted them to get in on the act at the earliest opportunity, and he discouraged red tape. There was no 'closed shop' for healers. When others outside the apostolic band were healing people, Jesus welcomed it, and turned aside the objections of the disciples (Lk 9:50). In the book of Acts, leaders like Stephen and Philip, who were not apostles, healed the sick, and Paul wrote about the gifts of healing in a general way in his letter to the Corinthians. The whole church should be a healing community, making room for the Head to continue to do what he began to do in the days of his flesh.

The dangers

When the Roman Catholic charismatics had their large Conference in Rome in 1975, the authorities were worried about what might happen. A memo was sent to the organisers that there should be 'no unseemly miracles'. We know what they were getting at, and they were not being unreasonable. They were concerned that there should be no undue sensationalism which might bring the church into disrepute. They were fearful of an Elmer Gantry style operation. But, on the other hand, it is difficult to see how sensations can be avoided altogether. Certainly the healings of Jesus caused many sensations. Crowds gathered very quickly, and Jesus was pursued by them wherever he went. A house was broken into, services in the synagogue disturbed, laws flouted, and the civil authorities had to ask him to leave one area at the instigation of the local pig breeders' association. How can you have miracles without sensations?

But Jesus never traded on his popularity, played to the gallery, or pursued sensations for their own sake. We find him increasingly withdrawing from crowds so that the flow of miracles diminishes, although he left his greatest physical healing (the raising of Lazarus), almost to the last. All kinds of theories have been put forward as to why Jesus usually discouraged those he had healed from talking about it. Many modern healers have their successes immediately in the glare of the floodlights and on the covers of their magazines. The cures are at once trumpeted for all to hear. That was not normally Jesus' style. The Son of God carefully avoided being made into a guru. He neither advertised his meetings nor his cures. He refused all attempts to be put on a pedestal, or to be made famous or wealthy by what he was doing. This may have been the reason why the synoptic gospels do not carry the story of the raising of Lazarus from the dead. Perhaps they wanted to avoid sensationalism for its own sake, and thought that the reporting of that miracle might obscure their primary purpose in writing, which was to describe the passion of Jesus and his glorious resurrection.

Eduard Schweizer in his famous book *Church Order in the New Testament*[6] puts forward the proposition that the documents of the New Testament reflect the changing scene in the early church. The earliest documents, with their stress on structure and order, are speaking to a strongly charismatic situation, inherently in danger of anarchy, and needing, therefore, bones to which flesh can adhere and which the Spirit can inspire. The later documents, particularly John's gospel and the Johannine epistles, address the need for a new release of the Spirit, in the face of growing authoritarianism in the church and an overemphasis on order, which was quenching the Spirit. Thus we can see John writing during this later period with a concern to recall the greatest of Jesus' physical healings – the raising of Lazarus from the dead. It may well be that by then some in the church were rejecting the stories about it which had been circulating from the beginning. Perhaps it was regarded by this time as an 'unseemly miracle'.

Triumphalism?

Although the gospels are not triumphalistic, they certainly record many triumphs of healing through the words and works of Jesus Christ. Sometimes the accusation of triumphalism, often levelled at those engaged in a 'signs and wonders' ministry, hides a poverty-stricken understanding of the place of miracles in the life of Christians. On the other hand we need to remember that the major part of the gospels is not given to healings, prominent though they were, but to the passion of Christ, and we need always to balance the relief of suffering in the records of healings the gospels give us, with the redemptiveness of suffering recorded in the trial and death of Jesus on the cross.

This is particularly important today, when there is a tendency in the western world to downgrade suffering as if it is something alien to life, and unacceptable to a believer in Christ. Jesus never told his disciples that they would escape suffering, rather the opposite. Malcolm Muggeridge wonders what would happen if we were able to eliminate suffering from the earth. 'What a dreadful place the world would be', he writes, 'I would almost rather eliminate happiness. The world would be the most ghastly place because everything that corrects the tendency of this unspeakable little creature

man to feel over-important and over-pleased with himself
would disappear. He's bad enough now, but he would be
absolutely intolerable if he never suffered.'

Having said this, it is also true that the church today could
do with some more triumphs, not least in its battle against
Satan and sickness. When victory came to Pastor Blumhardt
in a particularly bad case of demon possession, the church
bells in Mottlingen were rung for several hours. That's
authentic apostolic Christianity! But we should be on our
guard against false claims to power, the pursuit of sensations
for their own sake, wonders without signs, or a kingdom
without obedience to the King. The kingdom is here and now,
but it is also yet to come, and until these two aspects are
merged into one in the divine programme, we shall inevitably
be involved in pain and suffering.

The greatest healing of all

It would seem that when Jesus called Lazarus out of the tomb
he sealed his own fate. From then on, 'they took counsel how
to put him to death' (Jn 11:53). It was no longer a question of
whether they would do it or not, but *how* and *when* it would be
done. This miracle was the greatest of Jesus' healings, but
even it pales into comparative insignificance in the light of
what was shortly to follow, which resulted in history being
cleaved into two, and a stream springing up in Jerusalem
which was to immerse the world in its healing waters.

Our concentration on the healings of Jesus will be an
abortive exercise if we do not see the cross as the centrepiece
of it all. In London there once lived a famous family, the
Villiers. Their property was beside the Thames close to where
Charing Cross station now stands. Within a short distance of
the station there is an old gate which stood on the Villiers
estate. It is called the watergate. On it can still be seen the old
family arms with the motto, *fidei cotocula crux*, 'the cross is
the touchstone of faith'.

It is the cross, not miracles, which is the heart of the

Christian faith. It is the greatest miracle, the most sensational healing. Yet, the healings of Jesus were not a fringe benefit, but an important demonstration of that gospel message. In them we see mirrored the love and grace of God. We need such a mirror today. The signs and wonders are necessary today as much as then. A sceptical world needs to be convinced about a God who intervenes in our affairs. This book is dedicated to the same purpose expressed in the gospels, to make Jesus known so that people may believe in him. My prayer is that the healings of Jesus will do this for our generation as they did for those who lived in his.

Appendix: Word Studies

Wonders

The gospel writers use a number of words to describe Jesus' healing work. One of these is *teras*. This is the nearest equivalent to *thauma*. The closest we get to this word in the New Testament is in Matthew 21:15 where we have *ta thaumasia*, translated by the RSV 'the wonderful things that he did'. But the word normally (as in this text) describes the response of the crowds to Jesus' healings rather than the healings themselves (e.g. Mt 8:27; 9:33 and 15:31). Here we notice something of real importance. The word is never applied to healings except in conjunction with another word of which the most usual and striking is 'signs'. The term 'signs and wonders' occurs frequently in the New Testament, and in a variety of places (see Acts 4:30; 14:3; Rom 15:19; Mt 24:24; and Heb 2:4). In Matthew 24:24 it refers to false Christs and false prophets, so signs and wonders can come from other sources. The word 'signs', as we shall see, stands often on its own. *But the word 'wonders' never does.* Miracles are 'wonderful', but their significance only begins there.

Archbishop Trench draws our attention to the misfortune of being landed with the hot potato word 'miracle'. He regrets the prominence given to the words 'miracle' and 'wonders', like the Latin 'miraculum' and the German 'Wunder', because these words bring out 'only the accidental accompaniment, the astonishment which the work creates'.[1] The word 'miracles' does not penetrate into the depths of meaning which the biblical words employ. The fact that the evangelists never allow the word 'wonders' to stand on its own, is important. They wanted to draw the attention of their readers to the meaning of what had happened as well as the event itself. To understand the meaning would draw the reader to Christ himself, whereas the event, standing on its own, would only cause temporary excitement. Yet without the event there would have been no meaning. In passing it is worthy of note that the doctrine of the resurrection of Jesus Christ has the same principles built into it. It is not the empty tomb which is itself of major importance, it is Christ's resurrection which is earth-shaking. But without the empty tomb there would be no doctrine of the resurrection. Those who claim to believe in Christ's resurrection but deny the empty tomb are deluding themselves.

Having said all this, the word 'wonder' is there in the texts and serves a useful purpose. Archbishop Trench writes that it is calculated 'to startle men from the dull stream of a sense-bound existence . . . and to act as a summons to him that he now opens his eyes to the spiritual appeal which is about to be addressed to him'.[2] In the context of evangelism, Bishop Chitemo describes wonders as the 'bait' which catches the fish, and his experiences in Tanzania in recent years show how effective this can be. In the gospels and especially in the Acts of the Apostles the 'wonder' element arrested crowds of people, captured their attention at least momentarily and paved the way for an evangelistic message. No church today can afford to neglect this aspect of gospel preaching. Our society needs more not less sense of 'wonder'. There is little enough of it left. Scientists claim to have explained many of the mysteries of life. But is there not more to life than this? Has science even touched the hem of Christ's garment?

Signs

The healings of Jesus were also 'signs' that God was at work. The Greek word is *semeion*. The ethical and pastoral purpose of the healing is uppermost in the use of this word. The 'sign' aspect was there to lead the sufferer, the friends and relatives, the disciples and the crowds away from themselves and their immediate circumstances. It was there to act as a signpost which, although it does not mark the actual spot, does direct travellers and indicates where they are to go. Signs are intended to take people from the edge to the centre, from sense perception to faith, and from the present into the future. They were also seals of power, indicating the reality of the truth which was being preached. Thus in Mark 16:17 we read, 'these signs will accompany those who believe'.

They were also treated as credentials. Thus the Jews asked Jesus to prove himself by a 'sign from Heaven' (Mt 16:1). Paul also spoke of himself as having the 'signs of a true apostle' (2 Cor 12:12), just as God gave Moses two signs that he was the man chosen to deliver Israel (Ex 4:1–8f).

The word 'signs' was also used to describe other mighty works that Christ performed. A sign is not necessarily a miracle, but it plays an important part in describing one aspect of the healings of Jesus, and takes the significance of them beyond the healing itself. Its common use indicates that healings were a stepping-stone to something deeper and, therefore, more important. They had a higher purpose than the relief of suffering itself.

Mighty works

One of the commonest words used by the evangelists to describe the healings of Jesus is *dunameis*. Here we see an interesting comparison with *teras*. As we have already noticed *teras* primarily describes the effect that the healing had on the spectators. They 'marvelled'. In a secondary sense it is used to describe the healing itself – a 'wonder'. But the use of *dunameis* is the other way round. Primarily it describes the cause and in a secondary sense describes the effect it had on people. Jesus Christ was what Simon Magus blasphemously permitted himself to be called, 'that power of God which is called Great' (Acts 8:10). The word is used on several occasions and is usually translated in the RSV by 'mighty works', as in Matthew 7:22 and Luke 10:23.

These three terms – 'wonders', 'signs' and 'mighty works' occur three times in connection with one another although on each occasion in a different order (Acts 2:22; 2 Cor. 12:12 and 2 Thess 2:9). They describe different aspects of the same work of healing rather than different categories of healings. All of the healings of Jesus produced a response in people. They either marvelled, if they were open to what he was doing, or they were angry if they disapproved. It was impossible for anyone to be neutral or impassive. So 'wonders' described the effect the healings had on people. The word 'power' described what actually happened; the blind saw, the lame walked, the dead were raised up and the demons were put to rout. And the healings were 'signs' that they might believe in the one who had healed them.

Works

The simplest description of all was 'works' (*erga*), the word John is particularly fond of (Jn 5:36; 7:21; 10:25, 32, 38; 14:11, 12; 15:24). This is an important word because it points in the opposite direction to miracles and to the misuse of the term 'supernatural'. It suggests that the healings of Jesus were natural. In a sense the only miracle was the incarnation itself; everything else followed perfectly naturally. Jesus sometimes speaks as if what he was doing in healing the sick was ordinary, certainly natural. The healings of Jesus were a natural and normal result of his incarnation. They were the overflow of the coming together in human flesh of God and man. Trench calls them 'the fruit after its kind which the divine tree brings forth'.[3]

We are not, therefore, the least bit surprised that Jesus healed people. Our only surprise is that so many have been sceptical about this. As Trench comments 'it is no wonder that He whose name is "wonderful" (Isa 9:6) does works of wonder; the only wonder would be if He did them not'.[4]

Jesus assured his disciples they would do these works also, 'and greater works than these will he (the believer) do, because I go to the Father' (Jn 14:12). What was natural to the Son of God should be natural to us. But it has not been so during most of the history of the people of God since the first century. The church has constantly vacillated between extreme scepticism concerning miracles to becoming gullible and undiscerning to the point of encouraging magic and superstition.

Notes

Chapter 1

1. A. H. McNeile, *The Gospel according to St Matthew*, (Macmillan 1938) Intro. xv
2. T. Woolston, *Discourses on the Miracles*, 1729, 4
3. A. Schweitzer, *Geschichte der Leben-Jesu-Forschung* (Tübingen 1933) 415
4. Augustine, *Tractate on the Gospel of John* 17, 1
5. F. D. Schleiermacher, *Das Leben Jesu* (Berlin 1864) 203–244

Chapter 2

1. G. Gutierrez, *A Theology of Liberation* (ET, SCM 1974)

Chapter 3

1. McCasland, *By the Finger of God* (Macmillan, New York 1951)
2. J. Wilkinson, *Health and Healing*, (Handsel Press 1980) 26
3. J. Stewart, 'Neglected emphases in NT theology', *SJT* 4 (1951) 293
4. *ibid* 294, 295
5. *ibid* 298
6. *ibid* 301
7. J. D. G. Dunn, *Jesus and the Spirit* (SCM 1975) 47
8. A. Harnack, *The Expansion of Christianity*, vol 1 (Williams & Norgate 1904) 160, 161. On page 121 Harnack writes, 'Jesus says very little about sickness; he cures it.'
9. A. Richardson, *The Miracle Stories of the Gospels* (SCM 1942) 68

10 C. S. Lewis, *The Screwtape Letters* (Bles, 1942) *Preface* 9
11 Dunn 44
12 D. F. Strauss *The Life of Jesus Critically Examined* (ET, SCM 1973).
13 See H. van der Loos *The Miracles of Jesus* (E. J. Brill 1965) 394.
14 R. C. Trench *Notes on the Miracles of our Lord* (1889 14th ed) 164
15 For example L. Weatherhead, *Psychology, Religion and Healing* (Hodder & Stoughton 1951)
16 J. Wilkinson, *Health and Healing* (Handsel Press 1980).
17 See Loos 384, 396
18 O. Schmiedel *Die Haptprobleme der Leben-Jesu-Forschung* (Tübingen 1906) 114ff
19 See Trench 184 (footnote)
20 *ibid* 393, 394
21 Loos 410
22 A. Jeremias, *Babylonisches im Neuen Testament* (Leipzig 1905) 100
23 Quoted by Strack-Billerbeck I 722ff
24 Trench 368
25 Quoted by Trench 368
26 Quoted by Trench 370 (note)
27 F. Fenner *Die Krankheit im Neuen Testament* (Leipzig 1930) 54f
28 Loos 521
29 Augustine *Enarr.* ii in ps. 68.8

Chapter 4

1 Quoted by Trench 217 (footnote)
2 See Loos 426 note 5
3 Loos 428
4 Quoted by Loos 430 (footnote 6)
5 Trench 228

Chapter 5

1 A. Plummer, *Gospel According to St Luke* (ICC) (T and T Clark 1956) 237

2   L. Weatherhead 74
3   V. Taylor, *The Life and Ministry of Jesus* (London 1955)
4   A. M. Hunter, *The Work and Words of Jesus* (London 1950)
5   P. De Regla, *Jesus de Nazareth*, (Paris 1891) 251
6   Chrysostom *Homilies on the Gospel of John*, 62
7   See Loos 243–244
8   R. Bultmann, *The Gospel of John* (ET, Blackwell 1971) 407
9   A booklet is available from Captain Wilbourne, describing this
    story in some detail, c/o Church Army, Independents Road,
    Blackheath, London SE3 9LG. The story is also described in
    Invitation to Healing by Roy Lawrence.

Chapter 6

1   J. Calvin, *Harmony of the Gospels* commentary on Mk 8:23
2   Vespasianus VII
3   V. Donovan, *Christianity Rediscovered* (SCM 1982) 59–60
4   Loos 458–459
5   O. Cullmann, *Early Christian Worship* (SCM 1953) 37
6   C. H. Dodd, *The Interpretation of the Fourth Gospel*
    (Cambridge 1953) 138
7   *ibid* 319
8   Tertullian, *De Baptismo* 5
9   Chrysostom, *opp*. vol 3, 756

Chapter 7

1   Trench 354
2   S. Greydanus, *Commentary on Luke* (Amsterdam 1940)
3   A. Plummer, *The Gospel According to St Luke* (ICC)
    (Edinburgh 1956)
4   Strauss 99
5   Loos 515–516
6   *ibid* 532
7   Quoted in Trench 242
8   Augustine, *Sermon* 77.12
9   Bernard, *Serm* 3. *de anima*
10 Quoted by Loos 547
11 Bishop Hall, *Ev. Joh. tract* 16

12 E. R. Micklem, *Miracles and the New Psychology* (London 1922) 127ff

Chapter 8

1 Richardson 5
2 *ibid* 6
3 *ibid* 9
4 *ibid* 10
5 *ibid* 16–17

Chapter 9

1 H. Küng, *On Being a Christian* (Collins 1977) 226
2 A. Richardson, *Miracle Stories of the Gospel* (SCM 1941)
3 Quoted in Loos 4
4 *ibid* 7
5 Cicero, *De Divinatione*, II, 28
6 Loos 28
7 Quoted by Loos 28
8 E. R. Micklem, *Miracles and the New Psychology* (OUP 1922).
9 See Loos 32–33
10 *ibid* 34
11 Richardson 127
12 Augustine, *De Civitate Dei*, 21, 8, 2
13 D. S. Cairns, *The Faith that rebels* (SCM 1928) 246
14 K. Barth, *Church Dogmatics* (T + T Clark 1961) II, I, 540
15 C. S. Lewis, *Miracles* (Bles 1947) 15
16 Loos 46
17 *ibid* 47
18 Küng 236

Chapter 10

1 J. A. T. Robinson, *The Body* (SCM 1957) 11–16
2 Brown, Driver, Briggs 1022, s.v. *Shalom*
3 E. D. Burton, *Epistle to the Galatians* (ICC) (T + T Clark 1921) 425

4   Wilkinson 7
5   Three articles *The Times* August 8–10 1983

Chapter 11

1   J. R. W. Stott, *Christian Mission in the Modern World*
    (InterVarsity Press 1975)
2   J. Wimber, *Healing Seminar*, Vineyard Ministries Inter-
    national 5
3   L. Newbigin, *The Household of God* (SCM 1947)
4   David Barrett in his *World Christian Encyclopedia* (Oxford,
    1982) has included in his figures Charismatics as well as Pente-
    costals. He also has the most accurate figures available of Third
    World independent churches, most of which are charismatic.
5   Donovan 165–66

Chapter 12

1   Dunn 74
2   *ibid* 75
3   *ibid* 75
4   *ibid* 78
5   Wimber 21
6   SCM 1961

Appendix

1   Trench 2
2   *ibid* 3
3   *ibid* 8
4   *ibid* 8

Selected Reading

There is an absence of literature specifically on this subject. There are many books covering the general area of Christian Healing, but I have not included these in this list.

The only major book known to the author is by a Dutch writer H. van der Loos and is called *The Miracles of Jesus*. There is an English translation available published by E. J. Brill. Obviously there are innumerable Commentaries on the Gospels, but I have not listed them here.

R. C. Trench's *Notes on the Miracles of our Lord*, although published nearly a hundred years ago, has some good insights into the subject.

Those concerned about "alternative medicine" raised in Chapter 10, should read *The Holistic Healers* by Paul Reisser.

There will be a growing literature on "signs and wonders", and I have listed two recent books written by John Wimber and David Pytches as excellent material on this important subject.

I found Alan Richardson's book *The Miracle Stories of the Gospels* most helpful.

Dunn, J. D. G., *Jesus and the Spirit* (SCM, 1975)

Green, Michael, *I Believe in Satan's Downfall* (Hodder & Stoughton, 1981) 1973)

Green, Michael, *I believe in Satan's Downfall* (Hodder & Stoughton, 1981)

Harper, Michael, *Spiritual Warfare* (Kingsway, 1984)

Hunter, A. M., *The Work and Words of Jesus* (London, 1950)

Lewis, C. S., *Miracles* (Bles, 1947)

Loos, H. van der, *The Miracles of Jesus* (E. J. Brill, 1965)

Micklem, E. R., *Miracles and the new Psychology* (London, 1922)

Pytches, David, *Come Holy Spirit* (Hodder & Stoughton, 1985)

Reisser, Paul, *The Holistic Healers* (I.V.P., 1983) with Teri Reisser and John Weldon.

Richardson, Alan, *The Miracle Stories of the Gospels* (SCM, 1942)

Stewart, James, *Scottish Journal of Theology* 4 (1951)

Trench, R. C., *Notes on the Miracles of our Lord* (1889)

Wilkinson, John, *Health and Healing* (Handsel Press, 1980)

Wimber, John, *Power Evangelism* (Hodder & Stoughton, 1985)

Scripture Index

General Index